ENDING WAR

Ending War

The Force of Reason

Essays in Honour of Joseph Rotblat, NL, FRS

Edited by

Maxwell Bruce

and

Tom Milne

Foreword by Freeman Dyson

First published in Great Britain 1999 by
MACMILLAN PRESS LTD
Houndmills, Basingstoke, Hampshire RG21 6XS and London
Companies and representatives throughout the world

A catalogue record for this book is available from the British Library.

ISBN 0–333–76070–0 hardcover
ISBN 0–333–77482–5 paperback

 First published in the United States of America 1999 by
ST. MARTIN'S PRESS, INC.,
Scholarly and Reference Division,
175 Fifth Avenue, New York, N.Y. 10010

ISBN 0–312–22570–9

Library of Congress Cataloging-in-Publication Data
Ending war : the force of reason / edited by Maxwell Bruce and Tom
Milne.
p. cm.
Includes bibliographical references and index.
ISBN 0–312–22570–9 (cloth)
1. Nuclear disarmament. 2. Peace. 3. Conflict management.
I. Bruce, Maxwell. II. Milne, Tom, 1967– .
JZ5665.E53 1999
327.1'747—DC21 99–26118
CIP

This book is printed on paper suitable for recycling and made from fully managed and
sustained forest sources.

10 9 8 7 6 5 4 3 2 1
08 07 06 05 04 03 02 01 00 99

Printed and bound in Great Britain by
Antony Rowe Ltd, Chippenham, Wiltshire

For Joseph Rotblat

Contents

Ending War

Foreword

Freeman Dyson

Joseph Rotblat has devoted the greater part of his long life to the struggle to eliminate nuclear weapons from the earth. Unfortunately he was still in Poland in January 1939 when the possibility of nuclear weapons first became generally known. He was aware of the possibilities, but his voice was not heard in the public discussions of that year. If his voice had been heard, it is possible that history might have taken a different course. In 1939 a great opportunity was missed. That year was the last chance for physicists to establish an ethical tradition against nuclear weapons, similar to the Hippocratic tradition that stopped biologists from promoting biological weapons. The chance was missed, and from that point on the march of history led inexorably to Hiroshima.

In January 1939, a meeting of physicists was held at George Washington University in the city of Washington. The meeting had been planned by George Gamow long before fission was discovered. It was one of a regular series of annual meetings. It happened by chance that Niels Bohr arrived in America two weeks before the meeting, bringing from Europe the news of the discovery of fission. Gamow quickly reorganized the meeting so that fission became the main subject. Bohr and Fermi were the main speakers. For the first time, the splitting of the atom was publicly described, and the consequent possibility of atomic bombs was widely reported in newspapers. Not much was said at the meeting about atomic bombs. Everyone at the meeting was aware of the possibilities, but nobody spoke up boldly to suggest that questions of ethical responsibility be put on the agenda. The meeting came too soon for any consensus concerning ethical responsibilities to be reached. Most of the people at the meeting were hearing about fission for the first time. But it would have been possible to start a preliminary discussion, to make plans for an informal organization of physicists and to prepare for further meetings. After several weeks of preparation, a second meeting might have been arranged with the explicit purpose of reaching an ethical consensus.

Within a few months of the January meeting, Bohr and Wheeler had worked out the theory of fission in America, the possibility of a fission chain reaction had been confirmed by experimenters in several countries, by Rotblat in Poland among others, and Zeldovich and Khariton had worked out the theory of chain reactions in Russia. All this work was openly discussed and rapidly published. The summer of 1939 was the moment for decisive action to forestall the building of nuclear weapons. Nothing was then officially secret. The leading actors in all countries, Bohr and Einstein and Fermi and Heisenberg and Kapitsa and Khariton and Kurchatov and Joliot and Peierls and Oppenheimer, were still free to talk to one another and to decide upon a common course of action. The initiative for such a common course of action would have most naturally come from Bohr and Einstein. They were the two giants who had the moral authority to speak for the conscience of mankind. Both of them were international figures who stood above narrow national loyalties. Both of them were not only great scientists but also political activists, frequently engaged with political and social problems. Why did they not act? Why did they not at least try to achieve a consensus of physicists against nuclear weapons before it was too late? Perhaps they would have acted, if Joseph Rotblat had been there to urge them on.

Thirty six years later, the sudden discovery of recombinant DNA technology presented a challenge to biologists, similar to the challenge that the discovery of fission had presented to physicists. The biologists promptly organized an international meeting at Asilomar, at which they hammered out an agreement to limit and regulate the uses of the dangerous new technology. It took only a few brave spirits, with Maxine Singer in the lead, to formulate a set of ethical guidelines which the international community of biologists accepted. What happened at George Washington University was quite different. No brave spirits emerged from the community of physicists at the meeting. Instead of coming together to confront the common danger facing humanity, the two leading figures, Bohr and Fermi, began to argue about scientific credit. Fermi read aloud a telegram that he received during the meeting from his colleague Herb Anderson at Columbia University, announcing the successful verification of the fission process by direct detection of the pulses of ionization produced by fission fragments. Bohr objected to the claim of credit for Anderson, and pointed out that the same experiment had been done earlier by Otto Frisch in his own Institute in Copenhagen. Bohr was worried because Frisch's letter to *Nature* reporting his experiment had not yet appeared in print. Fermi was fighting for his friend Anderson and Bohr was fighting for his friend Frisch. Scientific priority was more important than common danger. The habit of fighting for priority, as prevalent in the scientific community of the 1930s as it is today, was hard to break. Neither Bohr nor Fermi was able to rise above their parochial concerns. Neither of them felt any urgent need to deal with the larger issues that fission had raised.

As soon as Hitler overran Poland in September 1939 and the Second

World War began, the chance of achieving a tacit agreement of physicists in all countries not to build nuclear weapons disappeared. We know why the physicists in Britain and America felt compelled to build weapons. They were afraid of Hitler. They knew that fission had been discovered in Germany in 1938 and that the German government had started a secret uranium project soon thereafter. They had reason to believe that Heisenberg and other first-rate German scientists were involved in the secret project. They had great respect for Heisenberg, and equally great distrust. They were desperately afraid that the Germans, having started their project earlier, would succeed in building nuclear weapons first. They believed that America and Britain were engaged in a race with Germany which they could not afford to lose. They believed that if Hitler got nuclear weapons first he could use them to conquer the world. Joseph Rotblat was marooned in Britain with his homeland destroyed and his wife in mortal danger. He had more reason than anybody else to be afraid of what Hitler might do with nuclear weapons.

The fear of Hitler was so pervasive that hardly a single physicist who was aware of the possibility of nuclear weapons could resist it. The fear allowed scientists to design bombs with a clear conscience. In 1941 they persuaded the British and American governments to build the factories and laboratories where bombs could be manufactured. It would have been impossible for the community of British and American physicists to say to the world in 1941, 'Let Hitler have his nuclear bombs and do his worst with them. We refuse on ethical grounds to have anything to do with such weapons. It will be better for us in the long run to defeat him without using such weapons, even it takes a little longer and costs us more lives.' Hardly anybody in 1941 would have wished to make such a statement. Even Joseph Rotblat would not have made such a statement. And if some of the scientists had wished to make it, the statement could not have been made publicly, because all discussion of nuclear matters was hidden behind walls of secrecy. The world in 1941 was divided into armed camps with no possibility of communication between them. Scientists in Britain and America, scientists in Germany and scientists in the Soviet Union were living in separate black boxes. It was too late in 1941 for the scientists of the world to take a united ethical stand against nuclear weapons. The latest time that such a stand could have been taken was in 1939, when the world was still at peace and secrecy not yet imposed.

With the benefit of hindsight, we can now see that if the physicists in 1939 had quietly agreed not to push the development of nuclear weapons in their various countries, there was a good chance that the weapons would not have been developed anywhere. In every country it was the scientists and not the political leaders who took the initiative to begin the nuclear weapon programme. Hitler, as we afterwards learned, was never seriously interested in nuclear weapons. The Japanese military leaders were not seriously interested. Stalin was not seriously interested until he was secretly informed of the size and seriousness of the American programme. Roosevelt and Churchill only became interested after their scientific advisors pushed them into it. If the scientific advisors had refrained from pushing, it is likely that the Second World War would have ended without any Manhattan Project and without any Soviet equivalent. It would then have been possible, as soon as the war was over, to begin negotiations among the victorious allies to establish a nuclear-weapon-free world with some hope of success. We cannot know whether this road not taken would have avoided the nuclear arms race altogether. At least it would have been a saner and wiser road than the one we followed.

In October of 1995, I was giving a lunch-time lecture to a crowd of students at George Washington University about the history of nuclear weapons. I told them about the meeting that had been held in a nearby building on their campus in January 1939. I told them how the scientists at the meeting missed the opportunity that was fleetingly placed in their hands, to forestall the development of nuclear weapons and to change the course of history. I talked about the nuclear projects that grew during the Second World War, massive and in deadly earnest in America, small and half-hearted in Germany, serious but late-starting in Russia. I described the atmosphere of furious effort and intense camaraderie that existed in wartime Los Alamos, with the British and American scientists so deeply engaged in the race to produce a bomb that they did not think of stopping when the opposing German team dropped out of the race. I told how, when it became clear in 1944 that there would be no German bomb, only one man, of all the scientists in Los Alamos, stopped. That man was Joseph Rotblat. I told how Rotblat left Los Alamos and became the leader of the Pugwash movement, working indefatigably to unite scientists of all countries in efforts to undo the evils to which Los Alamos gave rise. I remarked how shameful it was that the Nobel Peace Prize, which had been awarded to so many less deserving people, had never been awarded to Joseph Rotblat. At that moment one of the students in the audience shouted, 'Didn't you hear? He won it this morning.' I shouted, 'Hooray,' and the whole auditorium erupted in wild cheering. In my head the cheers of the students are still resounding.

About the Contributors

Oscar Arias, President of Costa Rica from 1986-1990, was the architect of the Central American Peace Agreement 1986-87. He received the Nobel Peace Prize in 1987.

Michael Atiyah, President of Pugwash Conferences on Science and World Affairs, was president of the Royal Society (1990-1995), Master of Trinity College Cambridge (1990-1997), and director of the Isaac Newton Institute for Mathematical Sciences (1990-1996). He received the Fields Medal in 1966.

Sissela Bok, philosopher, is a distinguished fellow at the Harvard Center for Population and Development Studies.

Maxwell Bruce is an independent consultant in public international law and a fellow at the Foundation for International Studies, Valletta, Malta. He was formerly a special fellow at the United Nations Institute for Training and Research (UNITAR).

Francesco Calogero is professor of theoretical physics at the University of Rome *La Sapienza*. He was Secretary-General of Pugwash Conferences on Science and World Affairs from 1989 to 1997, and has been Chairman of the Pugwash Council since 1997.

Freeman Dyson, physicist and author, is professor emeritus at the Institute for Advanced Study, Princeton, USA.

Vitalii Goldanskii is General Director of the N.N. Semenov Joint Institute of Chemical Physics, Russian Academy of Sciences. He was formerly a member of the Congress of People's Deputies of the Soviet Union.

Mikhail Gorbachev was General Secretary of the Communist Party and President of the Soviet Union from 1985 to 1991. He received the Nobel Peace Prize in 1990.

John P. Holdren is Teresa and John Heinz Professor of Environmental Policy and director of the Program on Science, Technology, and Public Policy in the John F. Kennedy School of Government at Harvard

University, USA. He is a member of President Clinton's Committee of Advisors on Science and Technology.

Sandra J. Ionno is Executive Director of Student Pugwash USA. Formerly she was a senior analyst at the British American Security Information Council.

Bruce Kent, peace campaigner, was president of the International Peace Bureau (1985-1992) and chairman of the Campaign for Nuclear Disarmament (1987-1990).

Robert S. McNamara was president of the Ford Motor Company (1960-61), US Secretary of Defense under John F. Kennedy and Lyndon Johnson (1961-68), and president of the World Bank (1968-81).

Tom Milne is a researcher at the London Office of Pugwash Conferences on Science and World Affairs, and a PhD student in the Programme of Policy Research in Engineering, Science and Technology, University of Manchester, UK.

Iwao Ogawa, eminent Japanese scientist, was the only nuclear physicist to witness the atomic bombing of Hiroshima on the ground – from a nearby island.

John C. Polanyi is a professor at the University of Toronto, Canada. He has published widely on arms control and peacekeeping and co-chaired the International Committee on a Rapid Response Capability for the United Nations. He received the Nobel Prize for Chemistry in 1986.

Anatol Rapoport, professor of peace and conflict studies at the University of Toronto, Canada, is author of numerous books including *Origins of Violence* (1989, second edition 1995) and *Peace: An Idea Whose Time Has Come* (1992).

Stanislav Rodionov is a senior scientist at the Institute of Space Research, Russian Academy of Sciences. He is a member of the Russian Committee of Scientists for Global Security.

Joseph Rotblat is emeritus professor of physics at the University of London and emeritus president of Pugwash Conferences on Science and World Affairs. He was the co-recipient of the 1995 Nobel Peace Prize with Pugwash.

Jasjit Singh is director of the Institute for Defence Studies and Analyses in New Delhi and a member of the National Security Council of India. He was formerly a fighter pilot and director of operations of the Indian airforce.

Herbert F. York is chancellor emeritus of the University of California at San Diego, USA. He was the first director of Lawrence Livermore nuclear weapons laboratory (1952-58), and US Ambassador and chief negotiator on the comprehensive test ban from 1978 to 1981.

Introduction

Vitalii Goldanskii and Stanislav Rodionov

This book celebrates the 90th birthday of Joseph Rotblat – one of the exceptional personalities of the twentieth century. Together with Pugwash Conferences on Science and World Affairs he was awarded the 1995 Nobel Peace Prize for efforts to diminish the part played by nuclear arms in international politics and, in the longer run, to eliminate such arms.

Joseph Rotblat, a man of extraordinary integrity, energy and enthusiasm, has been the heart and soul of the Pugwash movement of scientists since the first days of its existence. Born in Poland in 1908, he was working as an experimental nuclear physicist at Warsaw University when the startling news of the discovery, in Nazi Germany, of the fission of uranium shook the world's scientific community. Subsequent publications, as well as his own experiments and calculations, soon convinced Rotblat that the possibility of an explosive fission chain reaction was a matter of serious concern. In 1939, before the outbreak of war, he left Poland for England and joined such leading nuclear scientists as James Chadwick and Otto Frisch. Some four years later, he was recruited to work on the Manhattan Project at Los Alamos, New Mexico.

As soon as Rotblat concluded – as early as the end of 1944 – that Hitler's 'thousand-year empire' was headed for defeat before the Nazis could possibly develop an atomic bomb, he resigned from the Manhattan Project and returned to England. He had no intention of participating in the creation of weapons of mass destruction for use against Japan or for keeping the Soviet Union at bay. Instead, he shifted his scientific interests to radiology and nuclear medicine.

Ten years later, on July 9, 1955, the Russell-Einstein Manifesto (endorsed by Einstein two days before his death) was issued in London, signed, in addition to Russell and Einstein, by nine distinguished scientists, Joseph Rotblat among them. The Manifesto concludes:

> There lies before us, if we choose, continual progress in happiness, knowledge, and wisdom. Shall we, instead, choose death, because we cannot forget our quarrels? We appeal, as human beings, to human beings: Remember your humanity and forget the rest. If you can do so, the way lies open to a new paradise; if you cannot, there lies before you the risk of universal death.

The Canadian industrialist Cyrus Eaton made available his summer estate in the fishing village of Pugwash, Nova Scotia, Canada for a gathering of scientists in the spirit of the Russell-Einstein Manifesto. Twenty-two participants from ten countries convened at Pugwash in July 1957, and that was the beginning of the Pugwash Conferences on Science and World Affairs. Pugwash has since been credited with contributing to the development of several key international treaties controlling or prohibiting the testing, proliferation and possession of weapons of mass destruction. Just as important, Pugwash facilitated unofficial contacts between American and Soviet scientists and others during the Cold War years.

This book is a collection of essays written by friends and colleagues of Joseph Rotblat (and by Rotblat himself). They express original views on ways to move towards a nuclear-weapon-free world (NWFW) and a war-free world – the primary objectives of the Pugwash movement.

In an impressive introductory paper entitled 'The Force of Reason,' from which the book takes its name, Oscar Arias points to the fact that Costa Rica, his native country, is a military-free society. In 1998 Costa Rica celebrates the 50th anniversary of the abolition of its national army. Costa Rica is a living example of a nation that maintains its security not with arms but through respect for democracy, justice and international law.

The essays that follow are divided into two sections, dealing with eliminating nuclear weapons and ending war. The first essay is Rotblat's description of his involvement in the genesis of the atomic bomb. Working on the Manhattan Project had an enduring effect on his life. Not only did it cause him to change his scientific field – to work on the applications of nuclear physics to medicine, subsequently he devoted himself to arousing the scientific community and to educating the general public about the danger of nuclear weapons. Rotblat's motivation is explained in this passage, taken from his essay:

> After 40 years one question keeps nagging me: have we learned enough not to repeat the mistakes we made then? I am not sure even about myself. Not being an absolute pacifist, I cannot guarantee that I would not behave in the same way, should a similar situation arise. Our concepts of morality seem to get thrown overboard once military action starts. Our prime effort must concentrate on the prevention of nuclear war, because in such a war not only morality but the whole fabric of civilization would disappear. Eventually, however, we must aim at eliminating all kinds of war.

Mikhail Gorbachev – historically, the only President of the former USSR – regards the Pugwash initiatives as part of the arduous search for an end to the dangerous nuclear stalemate. He warns that we are on the threshold of a worsening of global problems that can be solved only through common, concerted efforts of all members of the global community. Gorbachev acknowledges that too often in the past few years, the national interests of some countries have been interpreted in the old way, with no regard for the context of our time and with no link to universal human interests. Once again, this calls for a new way of thinking 'which closely links national and global interests and values.'

Herbert York reviews the history of attempts to eliminate nuclear weapons and asks why has so much effort produced such limited results? He points out that an important factor is the lack of any serious response to treaty violations. He proposes the simultaneous establishment of three universal prohibitions: one on further proliferation, one on the threat of use, and one on the actual use of nuclear weapons. This would be combined with an agreed mechanism for enforcing them under the authority of the UN Security Council, analogous to the methods used so effectively in the Gulf War of 1990-91. He proposes in some cases the application of military force to destroy infrastructure dedicated to the design and manufacture of nuclear weaponry. And the prohibitions on use or threat of use have to be supported by political will to deal with even the most intransigent cases, using whatever means necessary, perhaps not precluding, in the most extreme circumstances, the realistic threat of retaliation from residual nuclear forces held under international control.

John Holdren asks whether pursuing a NWFW is too difficult, too dangerous, and too distracting – as NWFW sceptics argue that it is. The difficulties with a transition to a NWFW embrace the future of civil nuclear energy, linkages between nuclear disarmament and general and complete disarmament, and the matter of national missile defences. Dangers include cheating, breakout from an NWFW, and, arguably, a reduction in the restraints operating to prevent nations using biological weapons and engaging in conventional conflicts. The other worry is that pursuing a NWFW could distract attention from measures with more immediate benefits. Holdren argues that a commitment to zero and the accomplishment of some of the most important shorter-term arms control goals are inherently linked. His overall conclusion is that the prohibition of nuclear weapons is clearly desirable under appropriate conditions, and that the nuclear weapon states should commit themselves now to lead the way to achieving the conditions that will make prohibition feasible.

Francesco Calogero presents an interesting but debatable analysis of the well-known statement that 'nuclear weapons cannot be disinvented' – of importance, because this seems to be the main argument of those sceptical of moving towards a NWFW. Secret or classified information, focused on the construction of nuclear weaponry, is known only to relatively few people. This classified knowledge comprises written documents, computer codes, *etc.* and tacit knowledge embodied in people. If a decision were made to eliminate this knowledge, it would be easier to get rid of the written documentation than the expert knowledge. Therefore, in the context of a NWFW, the availability of large numbers of knowledgeable individuals would constitute a significant risk. Eventually the complete disappearance of all those who had a professional experience in operations with nuclear weapons will be a natural and permanent feature of a NWFW. But many interim difficulties will be avoided if the cadre of experts on nuclear weaponry at the time a NWFW is created does not include young people. Accordingly, Calogero proposes the introduction of a minimum age (of fifty) for granting the security clearances necessary for R&D activities on nuclear weaponry.

Iwao Ogawa introduces himself as the only nuclear physicist who saw, from the ground, the mushroom cloud over Hiroshima. He was about sixteen kilometres south of the centre of Hiroshima. This extraordinary experience is the strongest possible reason for viewing nuclear weapons as an absolute evil. He chastises the nuclear weapon states for continuing to consider nuclear weapons as necessary, and planning to retain their nuclear arsenals indefinitely. He regrets that the International Court of Justice avoided deciding whether the use or threat of use of nuclear weapons is lawful or unlawful 'in an extreme circumstance of self-defence, in which the very survival of a state would be at stake.' Ogawa also questions the US Stockpile Stewardship and Management Program, believing its budget is directed to developing novel weapons, based on research and development performed in military laboratories. He considers that any kind of basic research and development for military purposes is unacceptable.

Jasjit Singh reflects on human beings, their minds and the bomb. Nuclear weapons are universally acknowledged as the most horrible instrument of mass destruction and there is near universal agreement that nuclear weapons must be abolished: yet there is little movement towards such a goal. The role of nuclear weapons in the twenty-first century needs to be redefined. It is clear that changing the ideas and beliefs that currently justify nuclear weapons will be an essential part of our moving towards a nuclear-weapon-free world. Human history attests that what was once unthinkable can become the norm when a belief system alters. Two parallel paths have to be followed towards the abolition of nuclear weapons: a 'hardware' path – the deep reduction of arsenals and their elimination from national control; and a 'software' path – a process of changing the beliefs, attitudes and ideas supporting the use of those weapons.

The second section of the book begins with Robert McNamara's reflections on war in the twenty-first century. The twentieth century was the bloodiest in all of human history. The end of the Cold War did not conclude conflicts within or among nations: so the world of the future might not be different from the world of the past. But relations between nations will change dramatically. In the next century the United States will not have the power to shape the world as it chooses. New actors will play a larger role on the world scene, including Japan, Western Europe, China and several of the Third World countries (*e.g.* India, Brazil, Nigeria). In such a multipolar world, the need clearly exists for developing a new relationship among the Great Powers and between them and other nations. McNamara proposes a 'collective security' concept that would provide all states with collective guarantees against external aggression, codify the rights of minorities and ethnic groups within states, and establish a mechanism for resolution of both regional conflicts and conflicts within nations. McNamara warns of the high risk associated with the continued existence of nuclear weapons and gives details of the Cuban Missile Crisis in 1962, when the USA and the USSR were on the verge of nuclear war. He stresses that more political and military leaders are coming to understand two fundamental truths: that we can indeed 'put the genie back in the bottle,' and that if we do not, there is a substantial and unacceptable risk that the twenty-first century will witness a nuclear holocaust.

Anatol Rapoport deals with three philosophies of peace: pacifism, peacemaking and abolitionism. The pacifist sees the origin of conflict within the psyche of the human individual, the peacemaker in the interaction between pairs or groups of nations, and the abolitionist sees the roots of war in its infrastructure, the war-making institutions. The effectiveness of pacifism as an antidote to war is, Rapoport argues, limited. It is assumed that peacemaking can be made more effective by applying results of research on 'causes of war.' But peacemakers have in mind causes of war that are, in general, enormously complex. The abolitionist's concern is the necessary condition of war, that is, weapons. From the perspective of the abolitionist philosophy of peace, war appears as an institution that has remained virile by adapting itself to changing social environments. However, like all institutions, it can be assumed to be mortal. Abolitionists see their task as that of depriving the institution of war of further opportunities to survive by adaptation. Implementation of this task can be interpreted as 'war against war' that would have ideological side effects – changes in ways of thinking that Einstein regarded as indispensable for the survival of humanity.

Bruce Kent points out that many structures of peace are missing at the international level. We still lack a world criminal court with jurisdiction over states and individuals, and a system for controlling, let alone ending, the world trade in weapons. We have no effective pre-crisis international monitoring system, nor international legislation to define as criminal activities of scientists on the development of weapons of mass destruction. No international reward, respect or protection is given to those, like Mordechai Vanunu, who repudiate state secrecy in the interest of global security. There is no world police force of the kind envisaged by article 43 of the UN Charter. A culture of militarism finds expression in many different institutions. Even churches and universities often have close military links. The militarism in the mass media is all too clear. Kent concludes that the challenge to mankind is to build international structures within which international problems, war being one of the greatest, can be resolved.

Sissela Bok also discusses a 'war against war' using ideas that the philosopher and psychologist William James set forth in 1910: the need is to rechannel for constructive rather than warlike needs the energies, sense of honour, the discipline and loyalties that the most effective armies engender. For James, 'the moral equivalent of war' had to be a process, an engagement of human activities for constructive and peaceful purposes, rather than some elusive state of lasting peace that could only be envisaged as the end result of such a process. What James proposed was something akin to a domestic peace corps. More has been done, since James' day, to engage both men and women, old and young and of all nationalities, to serve across the world on ambitious tasks. But, as Walter Lippmann, once James' student, suggested, at times of crisis stronger preventive mechanisms, including international institutions, are clearly needed.

John Polanyi focuses on the United Nations and its developing role in peacekeeping. The UN Charter opened the door to collective actions in respect not only to conflicts between states, but to those within states. The prohibition of inter-state aggression is stronger now than ever before in history, but the prohibition of intra-state violence remains weak. Happily, in recent years the Security Council has identified the gross abuse of human rights within states as constituting a threat to the peace.

Sandra Ionno, a leader of the US Student Pugwash Group, represents the youngest generation involved in Pugwash activity. This generation has no memory on the Cuban Missile Crisis and to them the Second World War is ancient history. The TV movie 'The Day After' was their introduction to nuclear weapons. Yet this generation will be the bridge between two centuries and it needs to know, before making some bad choices, how to respond to the danger of new weapons of mass destruction and to Dolly, the sheep clone. It needs ideals, heroes and leaders.

The 'conscience of science' is discussed by Michael Atiyah who, having been president of the Royal Society for five years, knows from experience the meaning of this phrase. Scientists have a special role and obligations: if they create something, they should be concerned with the consequences; they understand the technical problems, and knowledge brings responsibility; and they form an international fraternity, able to take a global view in the interests of mankind. Scientists are often not free to use their expert knowledge to assist the public. Military and commercial secrecy are pervasive, even affecting so called 'pure' academic research. As a top priority Atiyah puts freedom of information and the elimination of secrecy. He urges scientists to cultivate the media, to counter ignorance, and to harness public opinion in constructive directions.

The concluding essay, Joseph Rotblat's 1995 Nobel Lecture, spans the whole scope of the book. It expounds, in accessible terms, Rotblat's main ideas on eliminating nuclear weapons, ending war, and the responsibility of scientists to contribute to these processes. If you read nothing else in the book, read this.

1

The Force of Reason

Oscar Arias

'Nothing else in the world ... not all the armies ... is so powerful as an idea whose time has come.'

Victor Hugo

Professor Joseph Rotblat has left us with a considerable legacy. He managed to ignite a flame from far within the frigid depths of the Cold War, which has gently grown over the past decade. The fire is large enough now that many leaders around the world have been drawn in and entranced by its glow. Radiant with peace and love for humanity, Professor Rotblat's blaze must be tended in the shifting and uncertain days ahead.

As we stand at the threshold of the twenty-first century, I sincerely hope that future generations may carry forward the tireless work of Professor Rotblat to its completion. And all those familiar with his efforts are aware that his mission will not merely end with the gargantuan task of nuclear disarmament. Indeed, his hopes consist in nothing less than to abolish war altogether. 'War must cease to be an admissible social institution,' stated the scientist in his 1995 Nobel Peace Prize acceptance speech. He went on to sound the dark tones of the Russell-Einstein Manifesto: 'Here then is the problem which we present to you, stark and dreadful, and inescapable: shall we put an end to the human race, or shall mankind renounce war?'

In the context of extreme circumstances – nuclear destruction – arose the need for extreme action. Yet today this message has lost not one degree of its urgency. For now that we have frightening technology in not only nuclear, but biological and chemical weaponry, the human race still teeters upon the cusp of self-destruction. And we will remain there until we abandon horrifying violence as a primary means to settle our differences.

But where do we begin? Which country will take the first step to renounce completely all weapons of mass destruction? Despite the startling progress both nations and individuals have made since the Cold War, and despite the momentous agreements signed, I do not expect a single nation to commit to such a radical disarmament policy. Not until a fundamental change is made in our realpolitik notions of security.

Indeed, an iron-clad concept still painfully lingers on, pronouncing that bulging arsenals are necessary for peace. Yet Professor Rotblat has shown us that playing precarious balancing games with nuclear stockpiles is simply not the solution for our present and future global security. It is my own hope in this brief essay to advance the full ramifications of my colleague's argument. That is, first we must succeed in eliminating nuclear weapons in the twenty-first century. Then, I pray that we may take on another seemingly insurmountable challenge: the abolition of military forces themselves – which lie at the root of large-scale human self-destruction and greatly contribute to world poverty.

As Professor Rotblat and I are both aware, statements such as these often provoke a deafening roar of criticism. Skeptics brand us as hopeless idealists, wide-eyed dreamers. And I for one admit that these claims may be true; for, our mission is a formidable one indeed. But am I alone in this hope? Let us consider the perspective of the world's majority – the poor. Are single mothers in Indonesia or street orphans in Egypt pressuring government leaders to increase military capability? Certainly not; the indigent of the earth are crying out for schools and doctors, not guns and generals.

Clearly, the world's militaries do not only account for human death and misery through the violence they perpetrate. They also shatter our hopes for human security. As we enter a new era, we must constantly remind ourselves that human security – in contrast to the traditional concept of security linked to military capacity and economic power – must be the ultimate goal of our actions. In quantitative terms, human security represents the degree to which human beings are protected from ignorance, sickness, hunger, neglect and persecution. It is the standard that dignifies human life. It is a child who is saved, a disease that is cured, an ethnic tension that is soothed, a dissident who speaks freely, a human spirit that has hope.

We can never have true peace without human security, and we can never have human security while we wage wars and build armies. Every soldier's gleaming uniform costs the world hundreds of dollars in medicine for the diseased. Every tank is the sad testimony of countless wretched men and women, without work or even a roof over their heads. Every missile tragically consigns innumerable malnourished children to painful deaths.

Let us consider the consequences of redirecting a small portion of world military spending toward investment in human security. In 1995, world military spending totalled nearly $800 billion. If, over the next 10 years, we redirected just $40 billion of those resources to fighting poverty, all of the world's population would enjoy basic social services, such as education, health care (including nutrition and reproductive health), clean water, and sanitation. Another $40 billion would provide all people on the planet with an income above the poverty line for their country.

The time has come to choose human lives over arms and armies. As a first step toward this end, a group of Nobel Peace laureates that I convened – Professor Rotblat notably among them – has unveiled an International Code of Conduct on Arms Transfers. The International Code of Conduct would govern all arms transfers, and stipulates that any country wishing to purchase arms must meet certain criteria, including the promotion of democracy, the protection of human rights, and transparency in military spending. It would also prohibit arms sales to nations that support terrorism and to states that are engaged in aggression against other nations or peoples.

Such measures, if diligently supported, may eventually bring us to a day when we no longer stand in peril of self-destruction. In such a military-free society, we would resolve our disputes through democratic forums and constant dialogue. As utopian as this may sound, my beloved Costa Rica is a living exemplar of such peace and democracy.

In 1998 Costa Ricans will celebrate the 50th Anniversary of the abolition of the National Army. On December 1, 1948, my predecessor José Figueres transformed the destiny of our nation, as he spoke the immortal words:

> The Costa Rican Regular Army ... relinquishes the key of these army barracks that they may be converted into a cultural center... We uphold the ideal of a New World in America. To this homeland of Washington, Lincoln, Bolívar, and Martí, we wish to say: Oh America! Other nations, also your children, gladly offer you their greatness. For our part, Costa Rica wishes to offer you, with all of its heart, now and forever, its love of civilization and democracy.

From that day forward, Costa Rica was set to follow a unique course. Our blessed nation would reserve its praise and honours for peace-loving women and men, not power-craving disciples of violence. We would learn to respect only the gentle force of reason, not the brute force of aggression.

I speak of my homeland not as a means to exclude others, but as a way to extend to the world an invitation to peace. We all have much to learn from this model of harmony in Central America. In these past five decades, all of the countries of Latin America have suffered through military dictatorship, except Costa Rica. Our liberties were never threatened, nor have we ever been burdened by oppression. The humiliation of a destiny governed by force and not reason is simply unknown in Costa Rica.

In these past five decades, all of the countries of North, South, and Central America have seen their students, farmers, and doctors fall victim to bloody conflict, except Costa Rica. Not one mother within our borders has mourned the death of her son or daughter in a war.

In these past five decades, minority groups in Costa Rica have never risen up in arms. For us, liberty is a permanent, living entity, and the right to vote is sacred. This is why we are not plagued by guerrilla warfare or internal strife. We have recognized that to achieve lasting peace, a nation must amass the power of democracy, tolerance, liberty, and solidarity – ideals which far surpass the potency of a nuclear warhead.

The current reality of Costa Rica is living testimony that security is not maintained with arms. It is maintained with a nation's prestige – which is the fruit of an undying respect for democracy, justice, and international law. Only a decade ago, these values prevailed through a maelstrom of conflict that engulfed the entire Central American region and involved both the USA and the USSR.

Truly, the East-West conflict was responsible for many lives and much havoc in Central America. The squalls of the Cold War rattled our bones and tore our homes apart. I remember a familiar Central American saying: 'the superpowers provide the weapons, and we'll supply the bodies.'

However, despite enormous pressures to continue fighting, in 1987 my fellow Central American presidents joined with me in Guatemala to sign the Esquipulas II peace accords – to end bloodshed and conflict in Central America once and for all. What greater test is necessary to demonstrate the superiority of reason over force and understanding over fear?

And now, 10 years later, we can see the outcome of the courage and perseverance of many. Central America is no longer at war. Every country in the region is a democracy; all have seen at least one peaceful transfer of power between freely-elected leaders. Indeed, thanks to a commitment to fair dialogue and indefatigable effort, the path towards demilitarization and enhanced civilian control in Central America has been paved.

Nothing in the world can now suppress Professor Rotblat's peaceful ideas – for their time has indeed come. Never before in recent memory have we had such an opportunity to construct a sustainable world peace. The Cold War's 'national security doctrine' has melted away. The Information Age brings us limitless ways to communicate and arrive at mutual understanding.

Yet the best reason to strive for peace is not because of these fortuitous present circumstances. The best reason is the reason which has always existed to wage peace: because it is our duty to humanity. In what Professor Rotblat calls 'our loyalty to humankind,' we must fight for human security – not military or economic hegemony.

In this celebration of one distinguished man of peace, our Professor Joseph Rotblat, and in the memory of another, my own countryman José Figueres, let us join together to ask the world to bid farewell to arms. Farewell to arms that stain the dignity of humankind. Farewell to arms that oppress nations. Farewell to arms that deny children their right to education. Farewell to arms that starve as many lives as they kill with violence.

Let us together work for a twenty-first century which carries Professor Rotblat's blazing torch of peace forward to all the nations, teaching us all to extol the force of reason and to reject the reason of force.

Eliminating Nuclear Weapons

2

Leaving the Bomb Project

Joseph Rotblat

Working on the Manhattan Project at Los Alamos was a traumatic experience. It is not often given to one to participate in the birth of a new era. For some the effect has endured throughout their lives; I am one of those.

This essay is not an autobiography; it describes only my involvement in the genesis of the atomic bomb. All extraneous personal elements are left out, but their exclusion does not mean that they are unimportant. Our hopes and fears, our resolutions and actions, are influenced by an infinite number of small events interacting with each other all the time. Because of this, each of us may react differently to the same set of conditions. The experience of every Los Alamite is unique.

At the beginning of 1939, when the news reached me of the discovery of fission of uranium, I was working in the Radiological Laboratory in Warsaw. Its director was Ludwik Wertenstein, a pupil of Marie Curie and a pioneer in the science of radioactivity in Poland. It did not take me long to set up an experiment to see whether neutrons are emitted at fission. I soon found that they are – indeed, that more neutrons are emitted than produce fission. From this discovery it was a fairly simple intellectual exercise to envisage a divergent chain reaction with a vast release of energy. The logical sequel was that if this energy were released in a very short time it would result in an explosion of unprecedented power. Many scientists in other countries, doing this type of research, went through a similar thought process, although not necessarily evoking the same response.

In my case, my first reflex was to put the whole thing out of my mind, like a person trying to ignore the first symptom of a fatal disease in the hope that it will go away. But the fear gnaws all the same, and my fear was that someone would put the idea into practice. The thought that I myself would do it did not cross my mind, because it was completely alien to me. I was brought up on humanitarian principles. At that time my life was centred on doing 'pure' research work, but I always believed that science should be used in the service of mankind. The notion of utilizing my knowledge to produce an awesome weapon of destruction was abhorrent to me.

In my gnawing fear, the 'someone' who might put it into practice was precisely defined: German scientists. I had no doubt that the Nazis would not hesitate to use any device, however inhumane, if it gave their doctrine world domination. If so, should one look into the problem to find out whether the fear had a realistic basis? Wrestling with this question was agonizing, and I was therefore glad that another pressing matter gave me an excuse to put it aside.

This other matter was my move to England, where I was to spend a year with Professor James Chadwick in Liverpool, on a grant to work on the cyclotron which was then being completed there. This was my first trip abroad, and the upheaval kept me busy both before the journey in April 1939 and for some time afterwards, because I spoke very little English, and it took me a long time to settle down.

Throughout the spring and summer the gnawing went on relentlessly. It intensified with the increasing signs that Germany was getting ready for war. And it became acute when I read an article by Siegfried Flügge in *Naturwissenschaften* mentioning the possibility of nuclear explosives.

Gradually I worked out a rationale for doing research on the feasibility of the bomb. I convinced myself that the only way to stop the Germans from using it against us would be if we too had the bomb and threatened to retaliate. My scenario never envisaged that we should use it, not even against the Germans. We needed the bomb for the sole purpose of making sure that it would not be used by them: the same argument that is now being used by proponents of the deterrence doctrine.

With the wisdom of hindsight, I can see the folly of the deterrent thesis, quite apart from a few other flaws in my rationalization. For one thing, it would not have worked with a psychopath like Hitler. If he had had the bomb, it is very likely that his last order from the bunker in Berlin would have been to destroy London, even if this were to bring terrible retribution to Germany. Indeed, he would have seen this as a heroic way of going down, in a *Götterdämmerung*.

My thinking at the time required that the feasibility of the atom bomb be established, one way or the other, with the utmost urgency. Yet I could not overcome my scruples. I felt the need to talk it over with someone, but my English was too halting to discuss such a sensitive issue with my colleagues in Liverpool.

In August 1939, having gone to Poland on a personal matter, I took the opportunity to visit Wertenstein and put my dilemma before him. The idea of a nuclear weapon had not occurred to him, but when I showed him my rough calculations he would not find anything scientifically wrong with them. On the moral issue, however, he was unwilling to advise me. He himself would never engage in this type of work, but he would not try to influence me. It had to be left to my own conscience.

The war broke out two days after I returned to Liverpool. Within a few weeks Poland was overrun. The stories that Hitler's military strength was all bluff, that his tanks were painted cardboard, turned out to be wishful thinking. The might of Germany stood revealed, and the whole of our civilization was in mortal peril. My scruples were finally overcome.

By November 1939 my English was good enough for me to give a course of lectures on nuclear physics to the Honours School at Liverpool University, but by then the department's senior research staff had disappeared: they had gone to work on radar and other war projects. I had, therefore, to approach Chadwick directly with an outline of my plan for research on the feasibility of the atom bomb. His response was typically Chadwickian: he just grunted, without letting on whether he had already thought of such a plan. Later I learned that other scientists in the United Kingdom did have the same idea, some of them with a similar motivation.

A few days later Chadwick told me to go ahead and gave me two young assistants. One of them presented a problem. He was a Quaker and as such had refused to do war work. He was therefore sent to Liverpool University for academic duties – but was diverted to work with me on the atom bomb! I was not allowed to reveal to him the nature of our research, and I had qualms of conscience about using him in such an unethical way.

The main idea which I put to Chadwick was that for the atom bomb the chain reaction would have to be propagated by fast neutrons; otherwise it would not differ much from a chemical explosive. It was therefore important to measure the fission cross-section for fast neutrons, the energy distribution of fission neutrons, their inelastic scattering, and the proportion of those captured without producing fission. It was also relevant to find out whether stray neutrons might cause a premature start to the reaction, which meant determining the probability of spontaneous fission of uranium.

We built up a small team of young but devoted physicists and used the cyclotron to tackle some of these problems. Later we were joined by Otto Frisch who measured the fast neutron fission cross-section for uranium-

235. I had the idea of using plutonium, but we had no means of making it.

As a result of these investigations, we were able to establish that the atom bomb was feasible from the scientific point of view. However, it also became clear that in order to make the bomb a vast technological effort would be required, far exceeding the manpower and industrial potential of wartime Britain.   A top-level decision was reached to collaborate with the Americans. And so I found myself eventually in that 'wondrous strange' place, Los Alamos.

In March 1944 I experienced a disagreeable shock. At that time I was living with the Chadwicks in their house on the Mesa, before moving later to the 'Big House,' the quarters for single scientists. General Leslie Groves, when visiting Los Alamos, frequently came to the Chadwicks for dinner and relaxed conversation. During one such conversation Groves said that, of course, the real purpose in making the bomb was to subdue the Soviets. (Whatever his exact words, his real meaning was clear.) Although I had no illusions about the Stalin regime – after all, it was his pact with Hitler that had enabled the latter to invade Poland – I felt deeply the sense of betrayal of an ally. Remember, this was said at a time when thousands of Russians were dying every day on the Eastern Front, tying down the Germans and giving the Allies time to prepare for the landing on the continent of Europe. Until then I had thought that our work was to prevent a Nazi victory, and now I was told that the weapon we were preparing was intended for use against the people who were making extreme sacrifices for that very aim.

My concern about the purpose of our work gained substance from conversations with Niels Bohr. He used to come to my room at eight in the morning to listen to the BBC news bulletin. Like myself, he could not stand the US bulletins which urged us every few seconds to purchase a certain laxative! I owned a special radio on which I could receive the BBC World Service. Sometimes Bohr stayed on and talked to me about the social and political implications of the discovery of nuclear energy and of his worry about the dire consequences of a nuclear arms race between East and West which he foresaw.

All this, and the growing evidence that the war in Europe would be over before the bomb project was completed, made my participation in it pointless. If it took the Americans such a long time, then my fear of the Germans being first was groundless.

When it became evident, towards the end of 1944, that the Germans had abandoned their bomb project, the whole purpose of my being in Los Alamos ceased, and I asked for permission to leave and return to Britain.

Why did other scientists not make the same decision? Obviously, one would not expect General Groves to wind up the project as soon as Germany was defeated, but there were many scientists for whom the German factor was the main motivation. Why did they not quit when this factor ceased to be?

I was not allowed to discuss this issue with anybody after I declared my intention to leave Los Alamos, but earlier conversations, as well as much later ones, elicited several reasons.

The most frequent reason given was pure and simple scientific curiosity – the strong urge to find out whether the theoretical calculations and predictions would come true. These scientists felt that only after the test at Alamogordo should they enter into the debate about the use of the bomb.

Others were prepared to put the matter off even longer, persuaded by the argument that many American lives would be saved if the bomb brought a rapid end to the war with Japan. Only when peace was restored would they take a hand in efforts to ensure that the bomb would not be used again.

Still others, while agreeing that the project should have been stopped when the German factor ceased to operate, were not willing to take an individual stand because they feared it would adversely affect their future career.

The groups I have just described – scientists with a social conscience – were a minority in the scientific community. The majority were not bothered by moral scruples; they were quite content to leave it to others to decide how their work would be used. Much the same situation exists now in many countries in relation to work on military projects. But it is the morality issue at a time of war that perplexes and worries me most.

I once came across a document released under the Freedom of Information Act. It is a letter, dated May 25, 1943, from Robert Oppenheimer to Enrico Fermi, on the military use of radioactive materials, specifically, the poisoning of food with radioactive strontium. The Smyth Report mentions such use as a possible German threat, but Oppenheimer apparently thought the idea worthy of consideration, and asked Fermi whether he could produce the strontium without letting too many people into the secret. He went on: 'I think we should not attempt a plan unless we can poison food sufficient to kill a half a million men.' I am sure that in peacetime these same scientists would have viewed such a plan as barbaric; they would not have contemplated it even for a moment. Yet during the war it was considered quite seriously and, I presume, abandoned only because it was technically infeasible.

After I told Chadwick that I wished to leave the project, he came back to me with very disturbing news. When he conveyed my wish to the intelligence chief at Los Alamos, he was shown a thick dossier on me with highly incriminating evidence. It boiled down to my being a spy: I had arranged with a contact in Santa Fé to return to England, and then to be flown to and parachuted onto the part of Poland held by the Soviets, in order to give them the secrets of the atom bomb. The trouble was that within this load of rubbish was a grain of truth. I did indeed meet and converse with a person during my trips to Santa Fé. It was for a purely altruistic purpose, nothing to do with the project, and I had Chadwick's permission for the visits. Nevertheless, it contravened a security regulation, and it made me vulnerable.

Fortunately for me, in their zeal the vigilant agents had included in their reports details of conversations with dates which were quite easy to refute and to expose as complete fabrications. The chief of intelligence was rather embarrassed by all this and conceded that the dossier was worthless. Nevertheless, he insisted that I not talk to anybody about my reason for leaving the project. We agreed with Chadwick that the ostensible reason would be a purely personal one: that I was worried about my wife whom I had left in Poland.

And so, on Christmas Eve 1944, I sailed for the United Kingdom, but not without another incident. Before leaving Los Alamos I packed all my documents – research notes as well as correspondence and other records – in a box made for me by my assistant. En route I stayed for a few days with the Chadwicks in Washington. Chadwick personally helped me to put the box on the train to New York. But when I arrived there a few hours later, the box was missing. Nor, despite valiant efforts, was it ever recovered.

The work on the Manhattan Project, as I said at the outset, has had an enduring effect on my life. Indeed, it radically changed my scientific career and the carrying out of my obligations to society.

Work on the atom bomb convinced me that even pure research soon finds applications of one kind or another. If so, I wanted to decide myself how my work should be applied. I chose an aspect of nuclear physics which would definitely be beneficial to humanity: the applications to medicine. Thus I completely changed the direction of my research and spent the rest of my academic career working in a medical college and hospital. While this gave me personal satisfaction, I was increasingly concerned about the political aspects of the development of nuclear weapons, particularly the hydrogen bomb, about which I knew from Los Alamos. Therefore, I devoted myself both to arousing the scientific community to the danger, and to educating the general public on these issues.

After 40 years one question keeps nagging me: have we learned enough not to repeat the mistakes we made then? I am not sure even about myself. Not being an absolute pacifist, I cannot guarantee that I would not behave in the same way, should a similar situation arise. Our concepts of morality seem to get thrown overboard once military action starts. It is, therefore, most important not to allow such a situation to develop. Our prime effort must concentrate on the prevention of nuclear war, because in such a war not only morality but the whole fabric of civilization would disappear. Eventually, however, we must aim at eliminating all kinds of war.

3

Working for a Humane Society

Mikhail Gorbachev

I know what war means – it marked my childhood years, and my father, a front-line soldier, told me about it. Later, during my years of political leadership in the Northern Caucasus and later in Moscow, I gained a very clear idea of what a third world war could mean. With the advent of nuclear weapons, mankind became mortal. The nuclear arms race, far from strengthening the security of the nations involved in it and of the world community, put their security in grave jeopardy. Mutual mistrust and suspicion increased the likelihood of an accident or technical failure triggering a nuclear apocalypse. On numerous occasions, both in our country and in the United States, radar mistook flocks of wild birds for a nuclear attack.

I regard the various Pugwash initiatives as part of the arduous search for an end to the dangerous nuclear stalemate. I recall in particular their warning in the early 1980s against newly fashionable strategies of 'limited nuclear war' and speculations about the 'advantages' of a nuclear first strike. I can say today that the courageous and well substantiated statements of Western scientists and opinion leaders supplied me and my supporters in the Soviet Union with fresh arguments in our efforts to effectively reduce the level of military confrontation, with the goal of eventually abolishing all aspects of it from relations among states.

It was a far-reaching long-term goal, based not just on the recognition of the Soviet Union's tremendous over-extension in the global arms race but, even more, on a broader view of things – a new understanding of the modern world and of our own country as an organic, though of course unique, part of it.

Viewing the world as an integral whole called for a new political philosophy, a new way of political thinking, and courage in practical action. The understanding of this gained ground in the government of the

Soviet Union during the years of my leadership. The challenge was to reorient the huge bureaucracies of the government and the party, to revamp the massive structures of economic management and, most difficult of all, to change the mindset of a society used to taking orders from above. Yet another task was to persuade the world that we were sincere and that our agenda was constructive, to overcome the deeply rooted inertia of mistrust and fear between the East and the West. How we did it, and what it took, is described in my Memoirs.

As for our efforts to reduce and abolish the nuclear danger, I consider it my duty to recall that the first steps that effectively scaled down the levels of nuclear arms on both sides were the fruits of the hard work and imagination of many people – scientists, diplomats, military and technical experts, and many others, with whom I often met, consulted and, on occasion, engaged in heated debate.

I devoted a great deal of time and effort to the key issues of nuclear arms reduction negotiations. This was necessary because the problems were new and complex but also, and even more so, because we had to contend with extremely powerful military-industrial organizations whose very rationale was to obtain huge amounts of public money to maintain military arsenals and turn out new, more sophisticated, weapons. The nuclear programmes of the United States and the Soviet Union consumed trillions of dollars.

One thing is important to note here, in order to counter ignorant or malicious speculation. While I took the initiative and assumed responsibility where necessary, I always acted in accordance with the constitution and policy decisions of the supreme bodies of our government, based on the country's national interests and taking into account the interests of the world community. I am not saying this in self-justification – there is no need for it – but to emphasize the need to address the issues of security, given their importance, in a very serious and authoritative manner.

We needed to develop realistic proposals to reduce the danger of nuclear war. We therefore emphasized verification – a broad and specific agenda of measures without precedent in the history of arms control. Given the West's deeply rooted mistrust of Soviet peace initiatives, this was not easy to accomplish. Indeed, during the first years of perestroika, high-ranking officials not just in the United States but also in countries such as the German Democratic Republic chose to regard it as little more than a propaganda exercise or 'a change of wallpaper,' a facelift.

The Reykjavik summit in October 1986 gave proof of the serious and far-reaching nature of Soviet anti-nuclear initiatives. This was the first time we proposed that both we and the United States cut in half all the components of the strategic nuclear triad – land, sea and air-based weapons. We were close to an agreement, which was thwarted mostly by the rigid commitment of the US president to his SDI programme, which jeopardized the principle of equal security. Nevertheless, Reykjavik demonstrated that an agreement was possible and that the new Soviet leadership was determined to address disarmament seriously. The US administration, too, showed a serious approach to the issues.

Two weeks after the talks in the capital of Iceland, I met with a group of leading international cultural and public figures convened at Lake Issyk Kul by our famous writer Chingiz Aitmatov. Among the participants in the Issyk Kul Forum were Arthur Miller, Alexander King, Alvin Toffler, Peter Ustinov, Omer Livanelli, Federico Mayor and Afework Tekle. We discussed the threats to humankind – nuclear weapons, threats to the environment, and other challenges. The question, as we saw it, was how to save our civilization and what responsibility fell on politicians, scientists and public opinion leaders to work to avert the threats to life on earth. The disturbing thought on everyone's mind was the aftermath of the Chernobyl nuclear disaster, which dramatically illustrated the possible consequences of 'local nuclear wars' and 'pinpoint nuclear strikes.'

Speaking at the Forum, I emphasized the primacy of universal interests and human values in today's world, at a time when the security of individual nations is so closely linked with international and global security. In 1986, this sounded like a revelation to many – and to some, like a heresy. I would say that today, there are few leaders of political thought who do not recognize this compelling truth. To me, the Issyk Kul Forum was a clear confirmation that public opinion both in the East and in the West would support dramatic steps towards a nuclear-weapon-free world.

The US-Soviet treaty eliminating INF missiles, signed on December 9, 1987, was the first such step. For the first time, an entire class of Soviet and American nuclear weapons was being abolished. By concluding this treaty, we were in effect removing a pistol aimed at us at point-blank range. Indeed, the misguided decision to deploy our SS-20 missiles in Europe had triggered NATO's countermeasures that put the most populous part of our country within range of Pershing-2 and cruise missiles. The INF Treaty was followed by further steps to cut the huge stockpiles of nuclear and other deadly weapons spawned by the Cold War.

The political and psychological atmosphere that began to shape international relations, the evolving trust among nuclear powers and, most importantly, the balanced and mutually verifiable arms reduction and limitation measures, prepared the ground for what, not long before, would have seemed a utopian breakthrough. By the late 1980s, the arms race was curbed and the Cold War ended. Confrontation was replaced by East-West co-operation.

The historic breakthrough was made possible by common efforts, and I recognize the contribution of my counterparts, such as Ronald Reagan, George Bush, Margaret Thatcher, Helmut Kohl, François Mitterrand, Rajiv Gandhi, Deng Xiaoping and Qian Tseming. But credit should also be given to scientists, writers and artists, who did so much to create a healthier international environment. Participants in Pugwash Conferences and their leaders were in the forefront of that movement.

We must not rest on our laurels, though. Recently, people have again grown concerned over the course of world developments. They are wondering why the international community is once again being divided by political and military barriers. They are asking whether a new hegemony is taking shape, and why the doctrines allowing a nuclear first strike are re-emerging.

Indeed, as Russia's high-ranking military officials have recently affirmed, the military doctrine of the Russian Federation, unlike that of the Soviet Union, allows for the possibility of being the first to use nuclear weapons in self-defence. It would be naive not to link such statements with the enlargement of NATO, putting the alliance in immediate proximity to Russia's borders. With renewed tensions in the Middle East, some people in the West have talked of the possibility of using nuclear weapons to strike Iraq.

All of this appears to mark a dangerous retreat from the model of international relations that emerged in the late 1980s in Europe and globally, an approach that rejected confrontation in favour of international co-operation, trust, partnership, and disarmament. That constructive and optimistic course was embodied in major international agreements, particularly the European charter signed at the Paris summit in 1990. It would seem, however, that these international agreements and the strategy they represent are now being neglected.

What is more, the long-term goal of the abolition of nuclear weapons, essential to global security, is also being forgotten. Has the world become so immune to the consequences of nuclear war that we can afford to stand idly by while others speak of the nuclear arms as the weapons of the twenty-first century, to be maintained and perfected? Is it not obvious that such talk can only encourage non-nuclear states to seek such weapons as their 'passports to the future?'

I feel that public opinion and the scientific community have not responded with enough strength and vigour to these dangerous shifts in politico-military concepts and practices. I salute those who have spoken out and particularly appreciate the fact that they include military leaders –

'generals for peace' like Lee Butler of the United States and Vladimir Belous of Russia, whom I know well. There is growing danger of global and regional environmental crisis, making even more probable heightened rivalries for resources and markets. Another source of concern is migration on an ever-increasing scale, a process that could get out of control.

We are, therefore, on the threshold of a worsening of global problems which, by definition, can only be solved through the concerted efforts of all members of the global community. This calls, again and more dramatically than before, for a *new way of thinking*. Its novelty lies in its ability to reflect correctly the interdependence of today's world, which closely links national and global interests and values, despite their pull in sometimes conflicting directions.

Too often in the past few years, the national interests of the United States, Russia, or any other country have been interpreted in the old way, with no regard for the context of our time and with no link to universal human interests. But surely it is in our common interest to preserve civilization and to have a world order allowing for the existence of all nations and states, regardless of their character, on equal terms and with dignity. A modern world order should make possible the development of democracy and social progress and the strengthening of freedom along with responsibility for the preservation of our civilization. By no means does this mean that national, group, corporate or other interests would disappear. Indeed, national interests could best be assured in a democratic world order. These and other questions of fundamental importance must, in my view, be clarified if we are to succeed in creating a new security architecture.

I am convinced that it is as true today as when it was first stated by the Palme Commission that in a mutually interdependent and interrelated world security must be common, indeed universal. No one nation would agree to have less security than another.

After the end of the Cold War, we are witnessing the advance of globalization, an increasing global interdependence. One of many examples is the recent financial upheaval in South-East Asia, which is having major repercussions throughout the world. For this reason alone, one has to be extremely careful when resorting to strong medicine anywhere. The lessons of the twentieth century are quite clear: dependence on force is ultimately counterproductive for the initiator of violence, leading to wars, bloodshed, and countless victims.

The twentieth century has also shown that history is not preordained, that there are always possibilities for alternative solutions. Let me cite two examples. The first one is the broad coalition against Hitler, which defeated fascism and nazism. The second one is what the leaders of East and West achieved in the late 1980s, when they rose above outdated ideological stereotypes and recognized the close interdependence of their national interests, thus putting an end to confrontation, the Cold War and the division of the world.

Unfortunately, soon after the victory in the Second World War, the leaders of East and West missed a historic opportunity for constructive co-operation. Instead, both sides pushed ahead with a race in weapons capable of bringing about an end to mankind's existence.

The process that began in the late 1980s has given people in our time a chance to move towards a new democratic world order in which all nations would be free to build their relations on the basis of equal rights and a balance of interests, without pressure, infringements or threats from any quarter. Reason and the conscience of our contemporaries must not allow this new opportunity to be missed. Of course, the world community and all nations that form part of it must be protected from rogue adventures, aggression and terrorism. But, on the eve of the twenty-first century, no member of the world community has a right to act unilaterally without regard for international principles and norms. After all, lynch law cannot be tolerated in any civilized society.

I have noted a remark made by Mr Li Peng, the Prime Minister of China, in the context of the discussion of recent events involving Iraq. The United States, he said, should be put on notice that no one can lay claim to be the world's leader. Instead, the USA can be one of the poles in the world, albeit an important one. I find myself in agreement with this view. Whoever tries to lead the world from one centre, whether Russian or American, is making a mistake. Of course, no such attempts on the part of Russia would be feasible at this time. Americans are more likely to be tempted by the role of a global policeman. But that, I am sure, would be bad for the United States itself, as most Americans, with whom I have had many opportunities to meet and talk, fully agree.

In the meantime, it appears that neither the United States nor Russia have a clear long-term course in world affairs or a vision of international politics and international security in the dawning century. Other countries, too, seem to be quite uncertain in this regard.

This brings me to two conclusions. First, there is a leadership gap in today's world. The reason is not that current leaders are inferior to their predecessors. The reason is that at the turn of the century there is a growing need for a qualitatively different kind of leadership – a concerted, united, democratic leadership. I believe that it is possible. But it is only possible if an appropriate political, spiritual and moral atmosphere prevails in the world.

My second conclusion is that creating and maintaining an atmosphere of constructive and action-oriented concern for assuring peace on a lasting basis in the twenty-first century, is a task of utmost importance and urgency not just for political leaders but for the entire world community. I am convinced that today, creative, courageous initiatives of scientists, artists and religious leaders of various faiths are no less important than in the years of the Cold War – particularly given the fact that the pace of the process of limiting, reducing and eliminating nuclear weapons is slackening.

The conscience of the world must not rest. Though there is no reason to panic, we do not have much time in which to act against a relapse into the past of terribly dangerous confrontation. As we are racing against time, it is becoming increasingly difficult to assure non-proliferation of nuclear weapons and missiles. Meanwhile, advances in science and technology could produce new types and kinds of weapons, even more difficult to control.

―――――――――――

Participating in marking the 90th birthday of Joseph Rotblat is an opportunity for me to salute a man whose dedication to saving mankind from the threat of nuclear self-destruction and whose intellectual and moral calibre I value and appreciate. I know from my own experience how much effort and strength is needed to move towards the goals that Joseph Rotblat and his colleagues in the Pugwash Conferences on Science and World Affairs so single-mindedly pursue. The movement is a source of hope for a triumph of reason and a humane society in a world which has lived through a century of unprecedented bloodshed, two world wars and countless civil wars and local conflicts. That is why I see the need for movements like the Pugwash Conference to get a 'second wind.' And that is why I wanted to join all those who pay tribute to the leadership of Joseph Rotblat and to his friends and colleagues. I thank him, and I salute those who are bringing fresh vigour to his great and noble cause.

4

The Road to Zero

Herbert F. York

The first attempts to eliminate nuclear weapons were made immediately after the first bombs were used. One of the earliest proposals for doing so was elaborated by Robert Oppenheimer with the help of I.I. Rabi and other colleagues, mostly veterans of the Manhattan Project. They wanted to eliminate atomic (nowadays read 'nuclear') weapons altogether while simultaneously promoting the development of atomic energy, which they all felt offered great benefits to mankind. They recognized the two could not be separated easily, so they invented an entirely novel scheme for doing so. In brief, they called for the creation of an international control mechanism which would own or otherwise control all steps in the chain of processes leading to any application of nuclear fission, including control of the mineral sources of uranium, the factories for processing nuclear materials, the laboratories engaged in developing them, and so forth. The then still brand new United Nations was thought to be the proper organization for accomplishing all this.

A committee chaired by David Lilienthal – who would soon become the first chair of the US Atomic Energy Commission – took up the idea, modifying it and elaborating it further. The Committee's membership included, among others, Robert Oppenheimer. Its report was passed to Dean Acheson, long a senior member of the American foreign policy establishment and later Secretary of State, who added some ideas of his own before passing it on to President Truman. History knows the result of this intellectual process as the Acheson-Lilienthal Report. The authors of this report were conscious of its radical and unprecedented nature, and of the criticism it would inevitably get from all who were not yet fully aware of just how serious the introduction of nuclear weapons into an unprepared world really was. At one point, in words which I believe were those of Oppenheimer himself, the Lilienthal Committee's Report says:

The program we propose may seem too idealistic. It may seem too radical, too advanced, too much beyond human experience. All these terms apply with peculiar fitness to the atomic bomb. In considering the plan, as inevitable doubts arise as to its acceptability, one should ask oneself 'what are the alternatives?' We have and we find no tolerable answer.

From '*A Report on the International Control of Atomic Energy,*' for the Secretary of State, by David Lilienthal *et al.*, March 16, 1946.

President Truman selected Bernard Baruch, a respected financier and elder statesmen, to be his representative for presenting the idea to the United Nations. Baruch added further changes of his own, including the idea that violators of the rules and regulations governing the control of atomic energy would receive 'condign punishment' and that such punishment or other essential actions of the control mechanism would not be subject to veto by the permanent members of the UN Security Council. Then as now, these permanent members greatly valued their right to veto whatever the Security Council might otherwise decide. It was, therefore, immediately obvious to most observers that these additions by Baruch had made the whole idea completely unacceptable to the Soviets, who felt outnumbered by the Western Powers, who themselves at first did in fact dominate the proceedings at the United Nations. (Two special bits of irony: In one of the earliest uses of the veto, the Soviets vetoed the Baruch plan which would otherwise have been adopted, and it was Baruch himself who first used the term 'Cold War' in a speech he gave in 1947.)

In retrospect, the plan was indeed '... too radical, ... too much beyond human experience.' Even without the particular – and later much criticized – additions by Baruch, the idea was, indeed, impossible for its time. It called for intrusions on sovereignty that were totally unacceptable to the Soviets, then under the absolute rule of Joseph Stalin, and, I believe, the US Senate would have found them unacceptable also, if such an agreement had been put before it for ratification in those times. During the next dozen years other proposals were put forward, but none could be realized under the international conditions then prevailing.

Finally, in 1958, after the death of Stalin made possible the first steps towards what would later be called détente. President Eisenhower and Chairman Khruschev were able to undertake the first serious negotiations since the failure of the original attempts immediately after the end of the Second World War. The first proposal that came close to succeeding concerned a comprehensive ban on all nuclear weapons testing.

Eisenhower's major goal was to take a decisive, though modest, first step down the long road leading to the eventual elimination of the nuclear threat still hanging over the heads of all of us. Earlier proposals for achieving some sort of control over atomic weapons were simply much too broad and much too difficult to verify – general and complete disarmament, for instance. Some required too much international intrusion on national sovereignty – the Baruch Plan is an example. Some were rejected because they seemed threatening in other ways – Eisenhower's 'Open Skies' proposal may have been in this category. In any event, all prior attempts to restrain nuclear arms had failed, and in 1958 a comprehensive test ban, being both limited in scope and relatively easy to monitor, seemed to offer a good chance for getting the whole process restarted.

The second major American purpose was to begin the gradual process of opening up the Soviet Union. From the beginning of the new negotiations, all parties seemed to recognize that some sort of international observation and inspection system would be needed for a comprehensive test ban and – by extension – for any other serious control over nuclear weaponry. And, since visitors of any kind to any part of the vast territory of the USSR were still few and far between, the possibility of opening up that huge country to any sort of international inspection, however modest, seemed to be a useful step in the right direction. In modern terms, Eisenhower's second purpose was greater transparency.

After what seemed like a promising start (for those times, anyway) these attempts also floundered, particularly because of insufficient transparency. The Soviet Union was by far the largest country in the world, and its political system gave the government near absolute control over its people and territory. These two factors combined with the long term hostility then prevailing in East-West relations made it impossible for most westerners to have much confidence in their ability to monitor what was going on inside such a huge territory. Nuclear explosions in the lower atmosphere (then the normal venue) might be adequately monitored because the winds always carried a fraction of the huge amounts of radioactivity they produced across international boundaries, but underground explosions were a different matter. Various schemes were devised for solving this latter problem, but they were always surrounded with controversy and none were ultimately convincing to those whose deep distrust of the Soviet Union led them to approach the issues with great caution. In most Western countries, the prospect of exposure by the press or dissidents made the prospects for successfully cheating on a test ban treaty extremely dubious at best.

The final result of these early test ban negotiations was the Limited Test Ban Treaty of 1963, during the Kennedy administration. It finessed the problem of inadequate transparency by banning only those tests that

took place in media where monitoring seemed promising, while ignoring
– and thus permitting – tests underground. Only in 1996 did it finally
become possible to elaborate an almost universally accepted comprehensive
test ban treaty (CTBT).

What has made this much progress possible? The answer is the
combination of a decrease in hostility (and thus fear) and a limited increase
in transparency, particularly in Russia and China, both elements being
consequences of the collapse of the Soviet Union and the end of the Cold
War.

In the meantime, in the mid 1960s, after the first five states had
already tested and deployed nuclear weapons, negotiations on a variety of
treaties designed first to limit and then roll back further developments and
deployments of nuclear weapons were successfully negotiated. They
include the various SALT and START treaties intended to severely restrict
the deployment of defensive systems and to limit the deployment of
offensive nuclear delivery systems, although to numbers that are still
extremely high in terms of the levels of death and destruction they can
cause. They also include restrictions on the deployment of nuclear
weapons in certain nuclear-weapon-free zones and outer space, and they
include the Non-Proliferation Treaty, which places its most precisely
drawn restrictions on just those countries that do not have nuclear
weapons.

Why has so much effort produced such limited results? What is
needed in order to achieve more far reaching and more meaningful results,
including really deep reductions and, eventually, the total elimination of all
nuclear weapons everywhere?

Two important factors in the answer to the first question are
insufficient transparency and the lack of any adequate response to
violations of treaty restrictions.

Adequate transparency is a relative term. As described above, what
was insufficient at the height of the Cold War is more than enough now
that the threat has diminished and the atmosphere of hostility has largely
evaporated. We still cannot know absolutely everything that is going on
in Russia, China, North Korea or Iraq, but most authorities think that we
can – perhaps after some further modifications in such things as
International Atomic Energy Agency inspections – know enough to support
the current treaty structure. But not, however, enough to go much further,
to deployment ceilings in the range of one hundred delivery systems, much
less their complete elimination.

The other important factor is the lack of any serious response to treaty
violations, the 'condign punishment' Baruch called for. This matter has
been largely ignored by the arms control and disarmament community,

activists and officials alike, mainly because any serious discussion of it up to now would have been seen as obviously hopeless and counterproductive. And indeed, Baruch was roundly criticized for trying to introduce the subject way back at the very beginning. When pressed, disarmament advocates, including myself, have had to fall back on weak responses: 'the opprobrium of international opinion' or, better, 'a detected violation could lead to the total collapse of the treaty, and since all the signatories evidently believed the treaty was in their mutual best interest in the first place, that alone deters violations.' This lack of strong response (condign means 'suitable,' 'fit,' or 'deserved,' but Baruch himself did not elaborate further) has all along led many politicians and statesmen to reject not just some particular treaty, but the whole treaty process. Their numbers have not been large enough to prevent the modest successes achieved to date; but really deep reductions, however, would be another matter, and this issue of inadequate response to violations would be enough by itself to generate opposition easily sufficient to stop them.

The remainder of this essay will focus on this latter issue, that is, the elaboration of the kind of response to violations that would make really deep cuts (to 100 or so and beyond) possible in the foreseeable future.

Specifically, the next to last step on the road to the total elimination of nuclear weapons should consist of the simultaneous establishment of three universal prohibitions: one on further proliferation, one on the threat of use, and one on the actual use of nuclear weapons, all combined with an agreed mechanism for enforcing them under the authority of the United Nations' Security Council, by means of prior authorizations and final actions analogous to those so effectively used in the Gulf War of 1990-91. The prohibition on further proliferation, once it is agreed, can in – very probably – all instances be handled successfully either by political and economic persuasion or, if those fail, by purely conventional means. In most cases it should also be possible to enforce the second and third prohibitions solely by conventional military means, but in some particularly difficult instances at least the realistic threat of nuclear retaliation – the threat that in the recent past provided the basis for nuclear deterrence – may be necessary.

The non-proliferation regime, now voluntary, must be made universal and compulsory. Such a change is clearly necessary if we are to move much further down the road to the elimination of all nuclear weapons. No doubt some will object that prohibiting some states from ever creating nuclear weapons while others continue to possess them – even if only in small numbers – is inherently 'unfair' and 'discriminatory.' This same objection was raised in connection with the NPT itself. There, it was solved in the first instance by including the famous Article VI in which the superpowers promised their best efforts to end and reverse the main arms race. At first they were slow to comply, but in the years since the Cold War ended the main arms race has in fact ceased, large reductions in stockpiles have been achieved both by treaty and through unilateral action, and the CTBT has been successfully negotiated. Something analogous to Article VI will be needed in this new case. For instance, the major nuclear states could commit to reducing their remaining stockpiles to no more than one hundred as soon as the conditions and arrangements described above are in place. Some might wish to go all the way to zero at the same time as these three universal prohibitions go into effect, and thus eliminate all unfair discrimination at the start, but I believe that would be going too far too soon. Indeed, I am convinced that the total elimination of all weapons, especially including those possessed by the current nuclear powers, can only come after the world has had some experience with arrangements of the sort I describe here, and not be coincident with them.

In most cases, the prohibition of further proliferation could very probably be enforced by no more than a realistic threat of universal and forceful political and economic sanctions. In some cases, however, the application of military force may become necessary to destroy the infrastructure dedicated to the design and manufacture of nuclear weaponry. But even in that case, the employment of a sufficient number of conventional 'smart weapons,' similar to but presumably more advanced than those used in the Gulf War, should make it possible to permanently eradicate such facilities with minimal casualties among persons other than those then at work in them. Many will find it more than a little unpleasant to contemplate such actions from the present quasi-peaceful perspective, but being prepared to do so is necessary if we are ever to eliminate the nuclear menace. Indeed, the existence of a firm and obvious political will to deal decisively with such extreme cases is the most promising way of assuring that they are unlikely to arise even once, and surely not a second time.

Combining the prohibition on further proliferation with the prohibitions on threat and on use has several merits. The principal merit is that all of these prohibitions are desirable, they are logically connected, and the means for enforcing them is in general the same. Another is that the second and third prohibitions do not suffer from the 'unfairness' handicap and thus the whole package should be much easier to sell than a free-standing compulsory non-proliferation treaty.

Enforcing the second and third prohibitions, those concerning the threat of use and the actual use of nuclear weapons, involve similar considerations. In these cases, too, the creation in advance of an obviously adequate and fully ready enforcement mechanism, backed up by the clear political will to use it, should, in most cases, be sufficient to accomplish the objective. Just as in the classic case of the Cold War, the primary reason for creating such a mechanism is to deter, not to counter, the prohibited actions. In both cases, for deterrence to succeed it must be credible. That is, it must be made obvious to any potential transgressor, to any renegade state, that the international community is fully prepared to deal with even the most intransigent cases by using whatever means may prove to be necessary.

In most instances, these 'necessary means' should be purely conventional, of sufficient size and involving the most modern weapons available, but not including any of the so-called 'weapons of mass destruction.' We must, however, be prepared to cope with the extreme cases, those in which, for whatever reason, conventional military forces alone are not enough either to deter or to respond to a prohibited act on the part of a renegade state. The civilized world must, therefore, continue to maintain some residual nuclear forces for as long as such possibilities can still become real. Like the conventional forces, these nuclear forces would remain in the possession of and under the immediate control of certain individual states – presumably those constituting the permanent members of the Security Council. However, the threat to use them and their actual use would be under the exclusive control of the Security Council and in accordance with the rules and plans established when the original arrangements for enforcing these prohibitions were made.

All this is, obviously, very different from the circumstances we have been living with for most of the last fifty years. Throughout the Cold War the United States and its allies openly reserved the right to initiate the use of nuclear weapons under certain extreme conditions. This policy was commonly referred to as extended deterrence. NATO, for example, made it widely known that it would reply to a massive ground attack on Western Europe with nuclear weapons if, as seemed all too possible, other means of resistance failed. Other states, while usually denying such intentions, very probably had similar plans for meeting similarly extreme contingencies.

Since the end of the Cold War, however, the attitudes of most leaders in the current overt nuclear states have changed radically. Formerly, such leaders commonly thought of nuclear weapons primarily as a solution to otherwise intractable security problems. Now the leaders of these same states generally recognize that the problems created by nuclear weapons in the hands of a growing number of other states override whatever advantages their own possession of them might still bring. As a result of these changes in their thinking, the leadership of the nuclear states is now, or soon will be, on the threshold of being ready to accept a universal prohibition on the use of such weapons. The situation is very different in some of the smaller – non overt – nuclear states. Typically smaller and militarily weaker than the current overt nuclear weapon states, their leaders evidently see the possession of nuclear weapons as the best, and sometimes the only means for levelling the playing field in a confrontation with a larger and otherwise more powerful state or alliance. The arrangements proposed here should make it possible for them to join the rest of the world in moving smartly towards complete elimination.

To summarize, each of these prohibitions would be enforced by means analogous to those used to initiate and win the Gulf War. The United Nations Security Council, in this instance well in advance of the need for any action, would pass resolutions spelling out each of these prohibitions and clearly declaring its intention to use whatever means may become necessary for their enforcement. The Security Council would at the same time make advance arrangements with all of its permanent members, and certain other major powers as well, to make the necessary means available. Again by analogy to the Gulf War, I do not imagine that the forces needed would either belong to the Security Council or be commanded by that body. They would, as in that earlier situation, continue to belong to, be maintained by, and be commanded by the individual states, but both the prior commitments and the final authority to use them would be in the hands of the Security Council. These forces would be primarily conventional in nature, but in order to be ready for a potential violation of the second and third prohibitions, those banning both the threat of use and the actual use of nuclear weapons, a reserve of nuclear weapons, again in the hands of an agreed subset of the members of the Security Council, and to be used only in the most extreme situations, would still be necessary.

To conclude, I return to the remarks quoted at the beginning of this essay. They were originally made more than fifty years ago, in what was in a great many ways a very different time. Although much has been accomplished in the meantime, the nuclear problem remains, unfortunately, unresolved. Nuclear weapons still pose a threat to humanity that goes 'beyond human experience.' We must develop and put in place a 'tolerable answer.'

5

Getting to Zero: Too Difficult?
Too Dangerous? Too Distracting?

John P. Holdren

There is remarkably widespread and growing agreement, at the end of the 1990s, on the desirability and feasibility of many nuclear arms limitation measures: on reductions in the nuclear forces of the United States and Russia going well beyond those prescribed in the START II treaty; on de-alerting measures that would increase the reaction time of nuclear forces from minutes to days; on a thoroughgoing revision of targeting practices in order to eliminate all consideration of massive attacks; on bringing into force the Comprehensive Test Ban Treaty and negotiating a comprehensive cut-off of production of fissile materials for weaponry; and on other measures to reduce the prominence of nuclear weapons in the foreign and military policies of the few countries that possess them and bolster the resolve of the rest to continue to refrain from acquiring them.

As remarkable as the extent of agreement on this range of restraints on nuclear weaponry, however, is the extent of the continuing lack of agreement on the desirability and feasibility of achieving a world free of nuclear weapons altogether – or, at least, on trying to achieve a nuclear-weapon-free world (NWFW) on any timescale of practical interest. Notwithstanding the spate of studies and statements, since the Cold War ended, by distinguished groups and individuals arguing that the time has come to address the elimination of nuclear weapons as a practical matter rather than merely a utopian goal, it seems apparent that getting to zero any time soon remains anathema to a majority of the people who populate the national-security establishments of the nuclear weapon states – or, at least, to a majority of those whose opinions matter most.

NWFW proponents argue that getting to zero is desirable to reduce the horrifying risks of intentional or unintentional use of nuclear weapons by the countries that now possess them, to prevent the proliferation of nuclear weapons (as well as chemical and biological weapons) to additional nations and to subnational groups, and to escape once and for all the vexing moral dilemmas of nuclear deterrence; and they argue that getting to zero has been made feasible by the end of the Cold War and by global trends towards democratization, co-operation, and interdependence. The NWFW sceptics, as I will call them, argue (with varying degrees of relative emphasis on the three points), that getting to zero is too difficult (many say impossible), too dangerous (both as a destination and en route), and too distracting from more promising arms limitation agendas to warrant pursuing it with any seriousness at this time.

In this chapter I address these arguments of the sceptics and weigh them against those adduced in favour of getting to zero by the NWFW proponents. At the end, I indicate where I come out myself on some of the major dilemmas and disagreements that characterize this topic. Before turning to these 'pro and con' matters, however, it is necessary to shed some light on differences concerning what zero amounts to – there is a wide range of interpretations about what elimination means, implies and requires – and it is to that task that I now turn.

Shades of Zero: Meanings, Implications, Requirements

The variations and ambiguities begin with the terms employed to describe what is being sought: the 'abolition' of nuclear weapons (a term often favoured by the more philosophical writers, such as Jonathan Schell[1]); their 'elimination' (the term usually favoured by diplomats, from the first UN resolution in 1946[2] to the Canberra Commission in 1996[3]); their 'prohibition' (a term favoured by those of legal bent[4] and, most recently, by the National Academy of Sciences' 1997 nuclear weapons study[5]); and 'nuclear disarmament' (which crops up in all kinds of treatments of the subject). Are there actually differences in meaning here, the sorting out of which could add precision or other insight to the discussion of 'getting to zero'? Are some of these terms more useful – by virtue of being more precise or appropriate to the use to which they are being put in this context – than others? I believe the answer to both questions is 'yes.'

Specifically, 'prohibit' in this context clearly means to 'forbid by authority of law,' that is, to make illegal.[6] This term is both unambiguous and clearly not synonymous with 'eliminate,' which means to cause the disappearance of something, to get rid of it entirely. Thus, for example, the United States imposed a prohibition on alcoholic beverages with the 18th Amendment to the US Constitution (lasting from 1919 to 1933), but these were far from eliminated. A prohibition on handguns, similarly, would represent an attempt to drastically reduce the numbers of these in use by making them illegal, although no one would expect it to quite lead to their elimination.

'Abolish' means to 'do away with wholly' or 'put an end to.' It embodies both the legal connotation of 'prohibit' and much of the sense of permanence and comprehensiveness of 'eliminate.' But it is more often (and some would argue more appropriately) applied to laws, customs, and institutions (such as slavery, capital punishment, or war) than to physical objects (such as nuclear weapons). Moreover, thinking about this word's most familiar usage, which is in relation to the abolition of slavery, suggests some ambiguity about whether complete effectiveness is implied: abolition certainly deprived slavery of its legitimacy, one presumes permanently, and disposed of the institution in its most conspicuous form; but still some forms of slavery persist (such as the selling of girls and young women into sexual slavery, which although illegal occurs quite routinely in a number of societies).

'Nuclear disarmament,' finally, is even more ambiguous: it can and often does mean merely reducing or limiting one's forces, not necessarily reaching zero. The usual approach to reducing this ambiguity is resort to more cumbersome (and nonetheless still ambiguous!) formulations such as 'complete nuclear disarmament' or 'comprehensive nuclear disarmament.'

These considerations figured in the preference expressed in the National Academy of Sciences' 1997 nuclear weapon study for the word 'prohibition' to describe an approach to the NWFW issue that ultimately could be accepted as both desirable and feasible. This choice has the attraction of avoiding both ambiguity and the common objection, made against 'elimination' or 'abolition,' that these goals are unattainable insofar as (a) there would never be certainty that every last weapon was gone and (b) the knowledge of how to make nuclear weapons – hence the possibility of reconstitution of nuclear arsenals – cannot be eradicated. Prohibition, as a matter of law, is certainly possible in principle; the main argument is about what it would actually accomplish.

There is also the question, of course, of exactly what is to be prohibited or eliminated in a NWFW. The candidates include, in order of increasing comprehensiveness and stringency:

(a)   nuclear weapons deployed with means for their delivery;
(b)   intact nuclear weapons in all conditions and locations;
(c)   (b) plus all nuclear weapon components;
(d)   (c) plus all military stockpiles of directly bomb-usable nuclear-explosive materials (separated plutonium and highly-enriched uranium);

(e)   (c) plus all stockpiles of directly bomb-usable nuclear-explosive materials, civilian and military;

(f)   (e) plus all facilities capable of producing directly bomb-usable nuclear-explosive materials;

(g)   (e) plus all nuclear energy facilities.

At each of these levels, moreover, there is a choice among: (i) prohibiting/eliminating these items altogether; (ii) prohibiting their possession by states but allowing possession by an international authority; and (iii) allowing their possession by states but only under dual control with an international authority. And there is the question of what other measures would need to accompany the nuclear prohibition, whatever its details, in order for it to be effective. That is: Is it necessary that chemical and biological weapons also have been convincingly eliminated? Conventional forces (or just the subset of these powerful enough to threaten the existence or independence of states)? All possibility of armed conflict between states? Would deployment of effective national defences against ballistic missiles help with a nuclear ban, or hurt, or make little difference?

A substantial part of the literature of 'getting to zero' has been devoted to the development of these diverse possibilities – and further combinations and variations of them – and to analysis and argumentation about their pros and cons.[7] Many of the relevant issues are treated here in the sections to come on the putative difficulties, dangers, and distractions of getting to zero, but three points need a bit of elaboration first as background for those discussions.

First, progressing through the foregoing hierarchy of nuclear prohibitions from (a) towards (g) brings successively greater barriers against the overt or covert reconstitution of the capacity to deploy and use nuclear weapons, longer time requirements for reconstitution starting from the decision to do so, and more protection against acquisition of nuclear weapons by subnational actors ... but also bigger obstacles to agreement and implementation. While, historically, most proposals to 'ban the bomb' have gone at least to level (d), there has been some recent attention to the possibilities of stopping at levels (a) or (b). Level (a), separating all warheads from their delivery vehicles, is of course not really banning the bomb at all but just a form of de-alerting; it would reduce some of the risks of accidental and inadvertent use, but would do little or nothing to reduce proliferation incentives or the perplexities of nuclear deterrence.

Level (b), which has been advocated recently by Michael Mazarr[8] under the label 'Virtual Nuclear Arsenals,' would ban intact nuclear weapons while allowing retention of nuclear weapons components. Intended as a position that might bridge the gap between abolitionists, on the one hand, and advocates of deep cuts and thoroughgoing de-alerting who have not been ready to embrace zero, on the other, this idea has been criticized as 'a fake zero' that would encourage countries to position themselves 'a turn of a screw' away from operational nuclear arsenals and would do little to de-legitimize reliance on nuclear weapons as instruments of national policy.[9] It appears that most proponents of a NWFW would accept the 'virtual nuclear arsenals' approach only as a temporary way-station on the road to a destination somewhere between levels (c) and (g).

Second, there has been a long-running debate within the NWFW community about whether achieving and preserving a world free of nuclear weapons requires placing constraints on civilian nuclear energy activities, that is, requires moving beyond level (d) to somewhere between (e) and (g). This issue, like so many others in the nuclear weapons arena, was already visited by Harrison Brown writing in late 1945.[10] A good account of the argument that verification of a NWFW is too hard and break-out from it too easy unless nuclear energy is banned along with the bomb was provided by Lovins in his 1977 book *Soft Energy Paths*.[11] The essence of this case is that the huge stocks and flows of directly bomb-usable material in nuclear energy systems that recycle plutonium make detection of theft or diversion of a few bombs' worth virtually impossible; and that, even in systems without such recycle, intolerably large break-out possibilities would still reside in a civilian nuclear energy system's large numbers of nuclear-skilled engineers and technicians, uranium-enrichment facilities readily adaptable to produce weapons-usable material, and potential for quickly building new facilities from scratch to extract plutonium from spent fuel.

These considerations have convinced many that, at the very least, a nuclear energy system compatible with a NWFW would need to be confined to the once-through fuel cycle, with all uranium-enrichment plants and spent-fuel storage under international control. Others argue that diversion-resistant closed fuel cycles yet to be developed and/or the co-location of all sensitive materials and facilities at internationally owned and guarded sites could also be consistent with a NWFW.[12] A quite comprehensive comparison of the pros and cons of different combinations of constraint and international control on nuclear energy in the context of a variety of interpretations of 'zero' nuclear weapons has been provided recently by Cochran, Paine, and Norris in one of the 'Background Papers' of the Canberra Commission.[13]

Third, beyond the question of whether international control of aspects of civilian nuclear energy would be a necessary condition for the maintenance of a NWFW, there is an even more fundamental question about whether confining possession or control of nuclear weapons themselves to an international organization might accomplish many if not all of the aims of a 'true' NWFW while being considerably easier to achieve. Most of the early ruminations on how to re-bottle the nuclear genie – both by the nuclear scientists who had developed these weapons and by the diplomats who pondered the matter in the early aftermath of the Second World War – were in fact focused on eliminating nuclear weapons from national arsenals and placing them under international control, not on eliminating them altogether.[14] These considerations presumably were influenced by the clarity with which the early weapons scientists, having just invented nuclear weapons, understood that they could not be un-invented.

In later discussions about complete elimination of nuclear weapons, the question of international ownership of an arsenal of nuclear weapons in a world in which nations had given them up re-emerged as a potential answer to the objection that a NWFW would be excruciatingly vulnerable to domination by a country that succeeded in concealing a small arsenal while others were eliminating theirs, or that subsequently reconstituted such an arsenal. An arsenal in the hands of an international body would provide the means for discouraging such cheating, assuming that the international organization in question was seen to be capable of acting if the need arose. The variant of 'dual key' control by an international agency and individual nation-states possessing nuclear arsenals has been suggested as a response to the concern that nuclear weapon states would not be willing to turn over complete control of such powerful weapons to an international body.

But ideas about international control of nuclear weapons, whether this control is exclusive or shared, continue to get mixed reviews. Among those observers who believe a NWFW is infeasible because of the reluctance of nuclear weapon states to give up this particular currency of status and power, many argue that these countries' transferring control of nuclear weapons to an international body is not significantly more likely than their agreeing to eliminate them altogether. Among those who *favour* a NWFW, moreover, there are many who feel that allowing an internationally controlled nuclear arsenal to remain after nations had renounced these weapons would be too large a concession to the proposition that threatening the use of nuclear weapons is a legitimate way to deter others from using them. (The differences of view on this point among NWFW proponents are on display in the 1993 Pugwash book *A Nuclear-Weapon-Free World: Desirable? Feasible?,* for example, in which some authors endorse the idea of an internationally controlled nuclear arsenal – at least as an interim measure – while others categorically reject it.[15])

Is Getting to Zero Too Difficult?

The issues just raised about whether a NWFW would need to include a ban on or international control of nuclear energy activities and whether nuclear weapons themselves might still be possessed, either temporarily or permanently, by international authorities are not only a matter of how a NWFW is defined and understood; they also relate importantly to the more fundamental question of whether a NWFW is feasible at all. It is just on this point of international control, in fact, that some of the arguments of supporters of a NWFW run into the greatest difficulty with the sceptics.

That is, for example, the supporters say 'A NWFW is only practical if civil nuclear energy activities are banned, too, or at least placed under international control.' To this the sceptics say 'Aha! You have just made clear why a NWFW is not feasible, because the countries of the world are never going to be willing to give up nuclear energy, or even to place under international control an activity as important to their economic well-being as nuclear energy is.' Or the supporters say 'A true NWFW would not allow any nuclear weapons at all, even in the hands of an international authority'; to which the sceptics respond 'Then your NWFW is certainly unattainable, because you have ruled out the only plausible means for dealing with cheating by individual nations.' (Of course, to supporters who *favour* retaining a nuclear arsenal under international control, the sceptics say – with even more force than in the case of civil nuclear energy – that countries will never be willing to cede this much power to an international entity.)

Certainly, many of the early thinkers who pondered the perils of nuclear weapons – notably the several groups of Manhattan Project scientists who struggled at the end of the Second World War with the implications of their invention[16] and the founders of the Pugwash Conferences a decade later[17] – reached the conclusion that for a ban on nuclear weapons to be really effective required not only unprecedented international powers of verification but also the abolition of war as a means of settling disputes between states. And quite a few of these thinkers pushed the argument to what seemed its next logical step, namely that the abolition of war could only be achieved in the context of 'general and complete disarmament' (GCD), enforced by a close-to-all-powerful world government. These ideas account for the persistent linkage of nuclear disarmament with GCD in most of the declarations, proposals, and treaty formulations put forward on this topic then and since. They also account for the view of opponents and sceptics of a NWFW that it is a utopian idea in the same class with GCD and world government ... and thus will never need to be taken seriously except in the almost unimaginable event that world government becomes a plausible proposition. Indeed, for the opponents of a NWFW, seeing it constantly linked with GCD and world government has undoubtedly been a source of great satisfaction – a way of reminding everybody that it will never happen.

Most proponents of a NWFW now argue, however, that there are worthwhile forms of a nuclear weapon ban that can be attained without waiting for the arrival of either GCD or world government. Much has happened, after all, since the 1940s and 1950s when these concepts seemed so closely linked. There is now considerable experience, for example, with a step-wise approach of outlawing the most worrisome (or most easily controlled) classes of weapons and activities first, rather than waiting for a comprehensive solution: banning atmospheric nuclear tests before a ban on all testing was possible; banning all testing before a ban on all nuclear weapon development work was possible; banning biological weapons before bans on chemical and nuclear weapons were possible; banning intermediate-range land-based ballistic missiles between the United States and the Soviet Union before a global ban on these missiles – or on all ballistic missiles – was possible; and so on. If banning nuclear weapons now looks like a sensible next step, the argument goes, there is no reason it needs to wait for GCD.

There is also much experience with building and operating a variety of global institutions that, while falling far short of constituting a world government, have been tailored to specific problems not likely to be adequately addressed by nation-states acting solely as independent entities. Institutions ranging from the International Atomic Energy Agency to the World Health Organization to the World Bank to the UN Security Council provide proof of the capacity of the world community to address complex global problems collectively when the need arises. And the trend in the direction of fashioning diverse institutions of governance to match the scale of the specific problems addressed – local, national, regional, global – seems likely to continue, suggesting that it may well be possible to craft an international institution (or upgrade an existing one) to deal with the challenges of creating and preserving a NWFW while appropriating only a modest piece of the traditional prerogatives of nation-states.

Whether a NWFW will prove to be too difficult in relation to the key problem of verification will of course depend on a combination of institutional arrangements and technical capabilities. Some analysts opposed to aiming for a NWFW insist flatly that such a thing could never be verified.[18] But technologies relevant to verification are constantly being improved, and few technologists would claim a crystal ball clear enough to know what will be possible with various forms of remote sensing combined with plausible degrees of in-country inspection in, say, twenty years ... not to mention fifty.[19]

On the institutional side, advocates of a NWFW beginning with Szilard in 1945[20] have pointed to the possibilities inherent in 'societal verification' – reliance on a sense of duty to humankind, reinforced by national laws that would be enacted as a part of the commitment of nations to a NWFW treaty, to motivate individual citizens who become aware of prospective violations of the treaty to report these to international authorities. (Joseph Rotblat has been a major contributor to the development and promotion of this idea and has recently described his view of it both in the Pugwash book *A Nuclear-Weapon-Free World: Desirable? Feasible?*[21] and in his Nobel Prize acceptance speech.[22]) It may be supposed that universal access to encrypted, anonymous communication with international authorities via the Internet – already close to a reality – will helpfully reduce the risks to 'whistle-blowers' even where laws encouraging such behaviour are not enacted or not respected by national authorities.

Another argument about the difficulty of achieving a NWFW has to do with a possible proliferation dynamic that might arise on the path from here to there. Those who make this point say that the large size of the US and Soviet/Russian arsenals has been one of the principal barriers to proliferation, insofar as most other countries could not hope to match these arsenals and would see little gain from creating nuclear forces that would necessarily be small by comparison. They also argue that allies of the United States and Russia falling under the protective 'nuclear umbrella' of these two countries' arsenals might be tempted, were the umbrella smaller, to acquire one of their own. In this view, then, any attempt by the United States and Russia to move down the path towards zero by drastically shrinking their own arsenals could backfire by lowering the 'entry barriers' to other countries' joining the nuclear club.[23]

This argument is at least partly undermined by the experience of nuclear proliferation to date: the third, fourth, and fifth nations to join the ranks of declared nuclear weapon states – the United Kingdom, France, and China – while not sufficiently reassured by the nuclear umbrellas of the United States (in the case of the UK and France) and the Soviet Union (in the case of China) to refrain from acquiring their own, evidently saw no need to compete with the size of the US and Soviet arsenals and were not therefore discouraged from going nuclear by their inability to compete in this way. They apparently concluded that whatever they needed in the way of nuclear deterrence did not depend on the relative sizes of arsenals but only on the ability to do an absolute amount of damage that any rational adversary would consider intolerable, for which an arsenal a fraction of the size of those of the United States and the Soviet Union would suffice.

Subsequent proliferation by the undeclared nuclear weapon states – Israel, India and Pakistan – likewise was not discouraged by their inability to compete, in terms of arsenal size, with the superpowers. The idea that a small number of nuclear weapons can act as an 'equalizer' in a world of power imbalances seems if anything to be growing stronger over time since the end of the Cold War, not weaker. That is indeed a difficulty on the path to a NWFW, but it is not one that US and Russian reductions are likely to make much worse. This, in any case, was the conclusion of the 1997 CISAC study of US nuclear weapons policy, which found that on balance the proliferation-suppressing effects of a large US arsenal were outweighed in the post-Cold-War world by the proliferation-enhancing ones.[24]

A last question I want to treat under the heading of the difficulty of a NWFW is whether the advent of effective national defences against nuclear-armed ballistic missiles would help or hinder progress towards a NWFW. Here one must first distinguish between the situation on the path to zero and the situation at the endpoint. With respect to the path, it is sometimes argued that such defences would help by devaluing nuclear weapons, making it easier for countries to agree to get rid of them. This position is undermined, however, by the great diversity of ways to deliver nuclear weapons other than by ballistic missiles. Unless effective defences are available against all of these means of delivery – from aircraft to taxicabs – devaluation via defences seems a weak effect. Quite the contrary, the logic behind the Anti-Ballistic Missile Treaty of 1972 holds that deployment of defences will inhibit reductions in the numbers of nuclear warheads mounted on missiles – thus discouraging progress down the path towards zero – because nuclear weapon states that continue to believe they need any nuclear weapons at all will want enough to be sure that they can overcome the defences. As the CISAC study argued, this logic seems no less compelling late in the reductions process (at low levels of nuclear forces) than early.[25] If zero had finally been attained, on the other hand, then deployment of missile defences could provide a benefit in reducing the gain that a cheater could expect from reconstituting a small arsenal, if these were going to be mounted on missiles. But even in this context of discouraging cheating in a world of zero, the availability of other, difficult-to-defend-against means of delivery might make the benefit of missile defences seem scarcely large enough to be worth the trouble.

Is Getting to Zero Too Dangerous?

Some sceptics question not only the feasibility of a NWFW but its desirability, arguing that even if it were possible to get there we should not want to do so. Their argument is that getting to zero would make the world even more dangerous than it is now, or more dangerous than it is likely to be in the future in the absence of attempts to get to zero. Some of the dangers they foresee arise on the path to zero, and others reside in the end-state – that is, in living in a world free of nuclear weapons.

The purported problems on the path to zero (besides those already discussed above under 'difficulty') have mainly to do with the possibility of instability – that is, with encountering a configuration of forces in which, with numbers of nuclear weapons smaller than today's, the incentives for resorting to their use in time of crisis could be larger than those incentives are today. This could come about, in principle, either because the smaller numbers might make the prospect of nuclear war seem less horrible than with today's arsenals, or because a combination of the smaller numbers and the interaction of counterforce capabilities on one side and vulnerability of the nuclear weapons on the other might make a pre-emptive first strike seem an attractive proposition.

These concerns cannot be dismissed lightly, but neither do they seem persuasive reasons not to try to get to zero. In the first instance, it will remain true throughout most of the path to zero (that is, all the way from today's tens of thousands of nuclear weapons down to the point where 'only' a few hundred remain) that the use of any substantial fraction of the stockpiles would destroy much of industrial civilization; thus, to this point, the barrier to nuclear weapons use posed by the magnitude of the potential consequences will not have been meaningfully lowered. And, even in a world where only a few tens of nuclear weapons remain, any rational leader will surely be restrained by the recognition that use of these would still be a catastrophe beyond any in human history. (That an irrational leader might not be restrained by this recognition is, of course, a problem with even larger potential consequences when the arsenals are larger, as today.) As for potential crisis instability arising specifically from vulnerability of residual nuclear arsenals to pre-emptive attack, this danger can and must be minimized – as the CISAC study[26] and others have argued – by careful shaping of the reductions trajectory to avoid counterforce/vulnerability problems at every step.

Another concern about the path to zero is that a world of low numbers of nuclear weapons – necessarily a way-station on that path – is a world in which these would be targeted against cities in order to maximize their deterrent value. If one accepts the claim of abolitionists that a major reason for doing away with nuclear weapons is the immorality of deploying weapons so indiscriminately and massively destructive of the innocent, then should one not resist moving to a situation in which these weapons are explicitly targeted to maximize the destruction of the innocent, rather than being mainly targeted against the nuclear weapons of the other side, as today? Perhaps the most compelling response to this concern is that the immense destructiveness of nuclear weapons renders almost immaterial the details of how they are targeted: there would be huge civilian casualties even from a 'pure' counterforce attack. Combined with the likelihood that any use of nuclear weapons, between two countries that both possessed them, would escalate to an all-out exchange, this means that the probable destructiveness of a nuclear war depends mainly on the sizes of the arsenals involved, not on any other details – a good argument for heading towards zero.

While it is sometimes also argued by NWFW proponents that targeting civilians in a world with small numbers of nuclear weapons is tolerable as long as this condition is only a temporary way-station on the path to a much better world, I would prefer to think it possible that the role of nuclear weapons would already be so greatly diminished in a world with arsenals much smaller than today's that the weapons would not be targeted at all. That is, they would be seen as a largely irrelevant remnant, en route to total disappearance, whose residual interim deterrent role if any were needed would be amply fulfilled by their mere existence, without need for specification of particular targets or even consideration of that unless and until some almost unimaginable reversal required it. (This is the situation that has been called 'existential deterrence,' wherein the existence of nuclear weapons exerts a certain deterrent effect that does not depend on any details of doctrine, deployments, targeting, or operational practices.[27])

The dangers generally associated with being in a NWFW – as opposed to the dangers of getting there – are mainly four: the danger of *cheating* (meaning that one or more nations or subnational actors clandestinely retain or reconstitute a number of nuclear weapons); the danger of *breakout* (one or more nations or subnational actors openly renounce the NWFW regime and re-acquire nuclear weapons); the danger that the absence of nuclear weapons will make the use of *biological weapons* more difficult to deter; and the danger that the absence of nuclear weapons will make *conventional conflicts* more likely and less restrained.

The problem of cheating is a matter of the incentives and barriers that bear on its probability, as well as a matter of the consequences that result if cheating occurs. The barriers depend on the adequacy of monitoring and verification – already discussed above under the heading of the difficulty of getting to a NWFW – as well as on the strength of the international norm against nuclear weapons and the consequences of being caught at cheating. The incentives depend on the benefits, to particular national or subnational interests, that are seen to derive from possessing some nuclear weapons in a world where few if any other national or subnational actors do. Inasmuch as I am dealing now with the dangers of being in a NWFW as opposed to the difficulties of getting there, it seems fair to assume for the purposes of this discussion that, a NWFW having been achieved, the monitoring and verification capabilities in place are at least quite good and the strength of the international norm against possession of nuclear weapons at least quite strong. The consequences of being caught at cheating in such a world could include a variety of economic, political, and military sanctions and countermeasures and would seem likely to be severe. (Of course the cheater might be a superpower, hence not very susceptible to such responses, but it is hard to see why such a power would feel it needed to cheat on the nuclear weapons ban at all.)

Not only would the barriers to cheating be considerable, but the benefits would seem to be quite modest. To get some benefit from the weapons – indeed, in order for their existence to affect the rest of the world at all – the cheater would need to reveal their existence; but, once revealed, they would be a rapidly wasting asset, inasmuch as other actors could use the ineradicable knowledge of how to make nuclear weapons to quite quickly acquire their own. In the variant of a NWFW in which these weapons had been banned from possession by states and sub-state actors but were retained in some numbers by an international body, of course, the benefit of cheating would be even less, perhaps negligible. And even in the absence of an internationally controlled arsenal, what would a cheater do with its temporary advantage? This question relates to the consequences for the world as well as to the incentives for the cheater. It is not easy to write a plausible scenario that amounts to much.

Similar considerations of barriers and benefits apply to the breakout problem, except that capabilities for verification and monitoring are less germane. Both for breakout and for cheating, then, the barriers would be considerable, the incentives and consequences limited. No one can show that cheating and breakout would be so unlikely and/or inconsequential in a NWFW as to be a non-issue, but neither does it seem persuasive that the risk associated with such developments – their probability multiplied by their consequences – should be regarded as comparable to the nuclear-weapon-related risks in a world from which such weapons had not been banned. (This question of 'Compared to what?' is of course crucial in contemplating the problems of a NWFW, and I return to it below.)

Another danger sometimes ascribed to a NWFW is that the absence of nuclear weapons would make the use of other 'weapons of mass destruction' – particularly biological weapons (BW) – more likely. (Chemical weapons usually get less emphasis in discussions along these lines, because they are clearly a threat of a lower order, against which it is harder to argue that a nuclear response would ever be warranted.) A variant of this position, which comes up in relation to the shorter-term issue of whether countries that possess nuclear weapons should declare unconditionally that they will not be the first to use them, is that the threat to respond with nuclear weapons is an indispensable deterrent to biological attack and should not be renounced through a no-first-use declaration.

As pointed out in the reports of the Canberra Commission[28] and the 1997 National Academy of Sciences nuclear weapons study,[29] however, there are serious liabilities of insisting that nuclear weapons are the only way, the best way, or even a desirable way to discourage the use of BW. First, the use of nuclear threats to deter BW use is likely to be of limited effectiveness, both because the source of a BW attack may be difficult to ascertain (making it unclear against whom to retaliate) and because the willingness of national leaders to cross the nuclear threshold in response to a non-nuclear attack may be doubted. Second, insisting that it is sensible to threaten nuclear retaliation against BW attack blurs the many distinctions between these two classes of weapons (among others, nuclear weapons are proven, predictable, and massively destructive of infrastructure and ecosystems as well as of human lives), which may actually encourage the retention or acquisition of BW by countries that think this provides an effective and inexpensive counter to the nuclear weapons of others. Third, if a country as powerful as the United States (for example) insists it needs nuclear weapons to counter BW threats, then many less powerful countries will be tempted to conclude that they have an even greater need for nuclear weapons for this purpose ... a clear prescription for nuclear proliferation.

While it is hard to doubt that the threat of nuclear retaliation can provide some deterrent effect against a nation that possesses BW and is contemplating using them, the cost of insisting on this function for nuclear weapons seems very high – the encouragement of proliferation of both biological and nuclear weapons and the relinquishment of the possibility of a NWFW. Given that there is already a global convention prohibiting BW, the NWFW proponents argue, it would seem better to work for strengthening its provisions (particularly for verification and safeguards) while trying to create the conditions for a prohibition on nuclear weapons as well, rather than assuming – and thereby guaranteeing – the failure of the BW ban while proposing as the 'remedy' the indefinite retention of nuclear weapons.

There is, finally, the danger that prohibition of nuclear weapons would, by eliminating a major source of restraint in international relations, 'make the world safe for conventional war.' Indeed, that the source of restraint provided by nuclear weapons today would be reduced in a NWFW is hard to doubt. The issue is the size and importance of the effect, which proponents of a NWFW argue is small and sceptics say is large.

The sceptics say that only the existence of nuclear weapons prevented a Third World War in the period from the end of the Second World War to the break-up of the Soviet Union 45 years later. NWFW proponents say that a determinative role for nuclear weapons in this outcome cannot be proven, and that many smaller wars and confrontations occurred in this period – including some that engaged the nuclear-armed powers – accompanied by large casualties and, in some instances, risks of escalation to nuclear war that should have been considered intolerable. It could easily have been a combination of good luck and good management, more than any immutable logic of deterrence, that got the world through this period without disaster. If it is conceded, moreover, that nuclear weapons at least reduce the chance of large scale conventional conflict between nuclear-armed powers, must one then concede also that a world of many such powers would be safer from major conventional war than the world of today? And what does this approach to preventing conventional war do to the probability of a *nuclear* war?

Proponents of a NWFW argue that the restraint against conventional conflict that nuclear weapons provide is bought at too high a price. They also argue that this source of restraint will be needed less and less as time goes on, because global economic integration, the intolerable destructiveness of even conventional conflicts, and other considerations will combine to make major war less and less likely altogether. The 1997 CISAC study, for example, made this point emphatically, listing among other relevant factors[30]

> the spread of democracy; the growth of information-based economic systems that do not depend on or benefit from territorial conquest; expanding economic interdependence and integration; the emergence of strong international financial and political institutions, such as the United Nations and the International Monetary Fund; the diffusion of global communications and shared culture, which limit the degree to which governments can control information and propagate negative images of adversaries; the advent of modern intelligence and surveillance systems that facilitate accurate assessments of military capabilities and which make surprise attacks less likely to succeed; the development of collective security arrangements, such as NATO and the Organization for Security and Cooperation in Europe; and, more recently, deployment by the Western powers of modern conventional armaments, such as precision-guided munitions, which improve the effectiveness of defenses against armored attacks.

The CISAC study also made the argument (as Schell had done in 1984[31]) that even the elimination of all physical nuclear weapons would unavoidably leave behind a residual deterrent effect against large scale conventional conflict, arising from the understanding that such conflict could lead to the reconstitution of nuclear arsenals and their use. This is a form of 'existential deterrence' that depends only on the existence of the knowledge of how to make nuclear weapons, which is ineradicable whether we like it or not; and it would reinforce the other factors mentioned as mitigating the concern that a NWFW would be prone to conventional war.

It has been suggested, on the other hand, that existential deterrence based on the possibility of reconstitution of nuclear arsenals might be less stable in time of crisis than deterrence based on arsenals already in place. The idea here is that a race to reconstitution of nuclear arsenals in time of crisis or conventional war could lead to incentives for the side that thought it was winning the race to use nuclear weapons first, while it had an advantage. Several questions suggest themselves. What would the first strike incentives really be in a world of only a few weapons? Could a few destroy the resolve of a potential adversary? Or destroy enough of the adversary's (and the world's) military capacity to rule out devastating retaliation? How would retention of some nuclear weapons in the hands of an international organization change the calculus? And how would these considerations vary as a function of numbers of weapons? These questions surely deserve more systematic analysis; but even as answers are sought it should be kept in mind that their overall importance will depend on other characteristics of a NWFW that, in consequence of the conditions that helped bring it about, could be so different from those of today's world as to make thinking about reconstitution, first strikes, and retaliation almost irrelevant.

Is Getting To Zero Too Distracting?

Many 'moderates' on the issue of a NWFW – people who are neither enthusiastic proponents nor committed sceptics – make the argument that, whatever the long-term attractions of a NWFW may be, pursuing this goal too energetically now poses the liability of distracting attention from measures with more immediate benefits (such as de-alerting of and deeper cuts in deployed nuclear forces, entry-into-force of the Comprehensive Test Ban Treaty, negotiation of a cut-off of production of fissile materials for weapons purposes, and so on). Such distraction could take two forms. First, a debate about banning nuclear weapons might, by focusing attention on a topic on which agreement is difficult, raise the level of contentiousness and confrontation in arms control discussions to the point where the goodwill needed to agree on potentially easier points is dissipated. Second, if the human resources at the disposal of governments for analysing and negotiating arms control are limited, spending too many of them in pursuit of a NWFW could mean inadequate resources for more immediate goals. Both concerns are captured in the question, 'Why spend time and effort disagreeing about the ultimate destination if we can agree on the direction we need to travel now?'

The argument for postponing attention to the pursuit of zero is undermined, say NWFW proponents, by the connections between a commitment to zero and the accomplishment of some of the most important shorter-term arms control goals. The most important of these linkages is with nuclear non-proliferation. The slow pace of proliferation during the Cold War, the achievement in 1995 of indefinite extension of the Non-Proliferation Treaty, and the signing of a Comprehensive Test Ban Treaty by most countries in 1996 are all good reasons for optimism; but all of this could be undermined sooner or later – and quite possibly sooner – if the nuclear weapons states do not finally make plain, now that the 'excuse' of the Cold War is long gone, that they do not mean to maintain their exceptional status as possessors of nuclear weapons indefinitely. And, while it is argued against this that the decisions of states about whether to acquire nuclear weapons depend far more on the local and immediate threats that they perceive than on what the United States and the other declared nuclear weapon states say about their long-term intentions with respect to their nuclear arsenals, the counter-argument is that the international norm against nuclear weapons matters and would be greatly strengthened by weapon-state declarations that they are committed to prohibition as a practical goal.

It needs to be remembered, in this connection, that decisions of potential proliferator states are likely to hinge on internal debates between 'hawks' and 'doves,' in which the balance could well be tipped in some instances by the clarity of the commitment of nuclear weapon states to get rid of these weapons. It also needs to be remembered, as the 1997 National Academy of Sciences study argued,[32] that

> the short-term and medium-term effectiveness of the global non-proliferation regime requires the full support and cooperation of a large number of non-nuclear weapon states in the maintenance of a vigorous International Atomic Energy Agency with the inspection powers and resources needed to do its job, the implementation of effective controls on the transfer of sensitive technologies, and the creation of transparency conditions conducive to building confidence that proliferation is not taking place.

Presumably, the commitment to these crucial, collective, non-proliferation efforts by states that are not potential proliferators themselves must eventually be eroded by continuing failure of the nuclear weapon states to commit to zero nuclear weapons for everyone ... not just for everyone else.

There is, finally, a more general argument supporting the idea of linkage between a commitment to prohibition and the attainment of shorter-term nuclear arms control goals. It is that nuclear weapon states' embracing the clearly defined, final goal of prohibition would invigorate the pursuit of all of the intermediate goals – deep cuts, de-alerting, and so on – by ending official support for the proposition that nuclear weapons have purposes that will persist indefinitely. This would immediately devalue the nuclear weapon 'currency' and hasten their marginalization in world affairs.

Conclusion

Let me use the conclusion of this essay to make completely clear my own positions on some of the key points at issue in the NWFW debate. To begin, I agree with the conclusion of the 1997 National Academy of Sciences study (in the preparation of which I was much involved) that[33]

> the potential benefits of comprehensive nuclear disarmament are so attractive relevant to the attendant risks – and the opportunities presented by the end of the Cold War and a range of other international trends are so compelling – that increased attention is now warranted to studying and fostering the conditions that would have to be met to make prohibition desirable and feasible.

I also find persuasive the argument in the National Academy study in favour of the term 'prohibition' to describe what is being sought: it has the merit of being unambiguous, clearly achievable, and consistent with what has already been achieved in the cases of chemical and biological weapons; and it can be seen as a practical means towards the ideal end of 'elimination' of nuclear weapons – an end which, as Calogero has pointed out,[34] is worth pursuing even if it can only be approached 'asymptotically.'

I would go beyond what the National Academy group as a whole was willing to endorse, however, in arguing that the nuclear weapon states should take the position already, today, that prohibition is clearly desirable under appropriate conditions, that the indefinite possession of nuclear weapons by any subset of states is clearly untenable, and that the nuclear weapon states therefore commit themselves now to lead the way to achieving the conditions that will make prohibition feasible before another half century has passed. I appreciate, but find ultimately unconvincing, the arguments that led the National Academy group, as well as the Canberra

Commission and the Stimson Center Project on the Elimination of Weapons of Mass Destruction,[35] to refrain from specifying a specific timetable. They are right to argue that the relevant variables are too many and the uncertainties too great to specify a timetable in detail. But an overall target is required to give meaning to the 'unequivocal commitment' to elimination of nuclear weapons called for by the Canberra Commission (or the 'serious commitment' called for by the Stimson Center group) and to give impetus to efforts to create the conditions that prohibition will require.

Any target will naturally be subject to revision – either more or less time might prove to be required – but there is at least a certain symmetry in the proposition that nuclear arsenals should be able to be built down in about the same amount of time that was used to build them up. (I proposed 2048 as the outer limit for getting to zero in a speech at the 150th anniversary conference of the American Association for the Advancement of Science in 1998,[36] where the theme was looking backwards and forwards fifty years. On the other hand, according to the Natural Resources Defense Council's tabulation[37] – the best unclassified source – global nuclear stockpiles peaked in 1986 at 69,500, declining subsequently to about half that number in 1998; if the entire build-down took only as long the build-up, 41 years, the world would be back at zero by 2027.) There is merit, in any case, in the idea that the target for achieving a prohibition should be within the lifetimes of many people now living.

In my opinion, the prohibition should include, at least, all intact nuclear weapons, all nuclear weapon components, and all military stockpiles of directly bomb-usable nuclear-explosive materials. I do not see need or benefit in allowing 'virtual' nuclear arsenals consisting of weapon components that could be minutes from assembly, except as a form of de-alerting not to be confused with a NWFW. The virtual arsenals approach fails to deliver the nonproliferation benefits of renunciation by the nuclear weapon states of their special status, and it fails to relieve the core moral dilemma of nuclear deterrence in the form of choosing to prepare deliberately for the mass destruction of innocents as a means for avoiding it. With respect to both these aspects, there is a crucial difference between the form of existential deterrence that would result from the ineradicability of knowledge about nuclear weapons (which is a state of deterrence arising from unavoidable circumstances) and the virtual arsenals idea (which is a form of the practice of deterrence); that is, knowledge-based existential deterrence is a permanent and universal condition associated with physical realities, requiring no conscious choices to maintain or exercise and not denied to some while allowed to others.

I believe it would be preferable for nuclear weapons, weapon components, and military stockpiles of directly bomb-usable nuclear-explosive materials to be banned altogether – that is, not only prohibited from possession by states but also not retained by any international organization – but I would favour allowing possession by an international agency as an interim measure, if allowing this could bring about a prohibition on possession by states earlier than would otherwise be possible. It is true that retention by an international organization would not represent as thoroughgoing a rejection of nuclear weapons and nuclear deterrence as a total ban would; but, as a way-station towards the latter, it would already achieve the nonproliferation benefit of erasing the distinction between nuclear weapon states and the rest, and it would take a great step towards the total delegitimization of nuclear weapons by making illegitimate their possession by states.

I think it is likely to be necessary, in order to get to and remain in a NWFW, that those aspects of civilian nuclear energy systems that lend themselves too readily to nuclear weapons production be foregone or placed under international management. The least problematic approach would probably be restricting reactors to once-through use of low-enriched uranium fuel, with the associated enrichment plants and spent-fuel storage facilities under international management. If economically competitive long-term energy sources that avoid fissile materials altogether are not available before the resources of uranium that are economically usable in once-through fuel cycles are exhausted, making recycle of plutonium appear necessary, this should be done only in internationally managed, integrated nuclear energy centres (with reactors and reprocessing and fuel-fabrication operations all at the same site), preferably using still-to-be-developed approaches in which the plutonium would never be completely separated from fission products.

I do not think that prohibition of nuclear weapons needs to await or be followed quickly by general and complete disarmament. Nuclear weapons are in a class by themselves in relation to indiscriminate, comprehensive, long-lasting destructiveness – the only weapons now known that could plausibly destroy all of civilization. If chemical and biological weapons can be banned without waiting for general and complete disarmament – as they have been and deserved to be – then so can nuclear weapons. Of course a world that has renounced armed conflict as a means of settling disputes would offer the ultimate security against the remobilization of any of these kinds of weapons; but even in the interim before this desideratum is achieved, the world will be better off banning nuclear weapons than continuing to permit them.

This brings us back to the question of 'Compared to what?' There are real difficulties on the road to a NWFW, and real dangers at the destination. But these are to be compared not to the perfection of a hypothetical hazard-free world, but rather to the risks and difficulties of continuing to live in a world from which nuclear weapons in the possession of states have not been banned and nuclear weapons in the possession of subnational groups cannot be ruled out. Here, it must be emphasized, the proper comparison is not just with today's conditions – with the hazards of accidental, erroneous, unauthorized, or other use of nuclear weapons by any of five declared nuclear weapon states and at least three undeclared ones – but also with the conditions likely to prevail in the future in the absence of decisive movement towards a NWFW. For the world cannot simply stay where it is. In the absence of a credible commitment by the nuclear weapon states to relinquish this special status on a timescale of practical interest, the number of nations choosing to acquire nuclear weapons for themselves is virtually certain to grow. Whether other factors affecting the probability of nuclear weapons use will improve rapidly enough to offset the adverse influence of a larger number of nuclear weapon states – and whether these improvements will apply everywhere that nuclear weapons appear – can be doubted.

Moreover, while there are a few voices arguing that a world of more nuclear weapon states will simply be a world of more robust and more comprehensive nuclear deterrence, no one can seriously argue that such deterrence will apply to the growing threat of nuclear bombs in the hands of terrorist and other criminal groups. That threat, which grows with the number of arsenals and bomb-material stockpiles from which criminals could obtain what they need, could well be the dominant nuclear threat in the next century; and not only is it greatly aggravated by the continued existence of national nuclear arsenals, but nuclear deterrence is likely to be useless against it (because terrorists and other criminals may not be locatable, or if locatable could not responsibly be attacked with nuclear weapons). It is therefore another reason for believing a NWFW is preferable to the alternative.

Would cheating and breakout be possible in a NWFW? They can be made improbable, but not impossible. Would the risks associated with these possibilities – that is, the consequences weighted by the probabilities – be greater than the nuclear risks the world faces today or is likely to face in the future without a NWFW? It does not seem so to me, for reasons adduced in the 'dangers' section, above, reinforced by a degree of optimism about potentially helpful technological changes: the evolution of monitoring capabilities (including internet-assisted 'societal verification') to improve the capacity to detect cheating or plans for breakout before they come to fruition; and the evolution of conventional force capabilities to improve the capacity to knock out rogue nuclear capabilities before they can be used (or, at worst, before they can be used more than once). If these capabilities are seen as insufficient in the context of the other incentives and barriers to nuclear weapons acquisition, keeping a small nuclear arsenal under international control as an interim step on the way to a true NWFW should be preferable by far to the hazards of a world with multiple nuclear arsenals in the hands of states.

To those who say that it is 'unimaginable' that verification of a NWFW could be good enough, or that sovereign states will ever voluntarily surrender control over nuclear weapons and nuclear-fuel-cycle facilities, I say these are failures of imagination. The rates of change in technology, in politics, and in international arrangements have been rapid in recent decades, and no one is smart enough to be able confidently to place limits on what may be achieved in a few decades more. It is entirely possible, in fact, that another decade or so of cuts in the US and Russian nuclear arsenals, de-alerting of the forces that remain, improved protection of nuclear explosive materials, a comprehensive cut-off of military production of these, and increased transparency and monitoring to go with it all will put in place a substantial part of the technical, institutional, and political ingredients that would be needed for a NWFW. Let us find out.

The failures of imagination that appear to afflict many opponents of a NWFW have never been a problem for Joseph Rotblat. An indefatigable and relentlessly effective pioneer among NWFW proponents, he has been imagining the ways to bring about a NWFW for decades, and has done more than anyone living or dead to bring this vision into being. It is has been a privilege to work with him and learn from him, and it is an honour to dedicate this essay to him on the occasion of this ninetieth birthday.

Notes and References

1.   Jonathan Schell, *The Abolition*, New York: Avon, 1984.
2.   United Nations, 'The United Nations and Disarmament 1945-1970,' United Nations, New York, 1970.
3.   Canberra Commission on the Elimination of Nuclear Weapons, *Report of the Canberra Commission*, Department of Foreign Affairs, Commonwealth of Australia, 1996.
4.   Jozef Goldblat, 'Making Nuclear Weapons Illegal,' in *A Nuclear-Weapon-Free World: Desirable? Feasible?*, ed. Joseph Rotblat, Jack Steinberger and Bhalchandra Udgaonkar, Boulder, Colorado: Westview Press, 1993, pp. 153-168.

5. Committee on International Security and Arms Control (William F. Burns, Study Chair; John P. Holdren, Committee Chair; Jo L. Husbands, Staff Director; and 14 others), *The Future of U.S. Nuclear Weapons Policy,* Washington D.C.: National Academy Press, 1997.

6. The definitions relied upon here are from *Webster's Third New International Dictionary (Unabridged),* Springfield, MA: Merriam, 1966; and *The Random House Dictionary of the English Language (The Unabridged Edition),* New York: Random House, 1979.

7. See, especially, Harrison Brown's prescient book, *Must Destruction Be Our Destiny?,* New York: Simon and Schuster, 1946; Jonathan Schell, *The Abolition; A Nuclear-Weapon-Free World ...,* ed. Rotblat, Steinberger and Udgaonkar; *Report of the Canberra Commission: Background Papers,* under the same imprint and date as the main report, containing analyses prepared for the Commission by a wide array of consultants; and Steven Miller's recent précis 'Nuclear Weapons: The Abolitionist Upsurge,' International Institute for Stategic Studies, *Strategic Survey 1998-99,* Oxford University Press, 1998.

8. Michael J. Mazarr, 'Virtual Nuclear Arsenals,' *Survival,* 37:3, pp. 7-26.

9. For an extended discussion, see Jonathan Schell's new essay on abolition, 'The Gift of Time,' *The Nation,* February 2/9, 1998, pp. 9-60.

10. Harrison Brown, *Must Destruction Be Our Destiny?*

11. Amory B. Lovins, *Soft Energy Parths: Toward a Durable Peace,* Cambridge, MA: Ballinger, 1977. See especially chapter 11, 'Rebottling the Nuclear Genie.'

12. Wolf Haefele, 'Energy from Nuclear Power,' *Scientific American,* September 1990, pp. 136-144.

13. Christoper E. Paine, Thomas B. Cochran, and Robert S. Norris, 'International Arrangements for the Transition to a Nuclear Weapon Free World,' in *Background Papers,* Canberra Commission on the Elimination of Nuclear Weapons, pp. 141-155.

14. Joseph Rotblat, 'Past Attempts to Abolish Nuclear Weapons,' in *A Nuclear-Weapon-Free World ...,* ed. Rotblat, Steinberger and Udgaonkar, pp. 17-32; William Lanouette with Bela Szilard, *Genius in the Shadows,* New York: Scribner's, 1992; Harrison Brown, *Must Destruction Be Our Destiny?*; United Nations, 'The United Nations and Disarmament 1945-1970.'

15. *A Nuclear-Weapon-Free World ...,* ed. Rotblat, Steinberger and Udgaonkar: contrast chapter 8 (James Leonard, Martin Kaplan and Benjamin Sanders, 'Verification and Enforcement in a NWFW') and chapter 13 (Francesco Calogero, 'An Asymptotic Approach to a NWFW') with chapter 11 (Richard Garwin, 'Nuclear Weapons for the United Nations') and chapter 12 (Vitalii Goldanskii and Stanislav Rodionov, 'An International Nuclear Security Force').

16. Joseph Rotblat, 'Past Attempts to Abolish Nuclear Weapons;' William Lanouette with Bela Szilard, *Genius in the Shadows*; Harrison Brown, *Must Destruction Be Our Destiny?*

17. The Russell-Einstein Manifesto, which can be found at http://www.qmw.ac.uk/pugwash/archive/manifesto.html; Joseph Rotblat, *Pugwash: The First Ten Years,* London: Heinemann, 1967.

18. Richard Perle, testimony before the Subcommittee on International Security, Proliferation, and Federal Services, February 12, 1997, available on the Stimson Center website at http://www.stimson.org/forum/perle.htm

19. Theodore Taylor, 'Technological Problems of Verification,' in *A Nuclear-Weapon-Free World ...*, Rotblat, Steinberger and Udgaonkar eds, pp. 63-82; Christopher E. Paine, Thomas B. Cochran, and Robert S. Norris, 'Techniques and Procedures for Verifying Nuclear Weapons Elimination,' *Background Papers*, Canberra Commission on the Elimination of Nuclear Weapons, pp. 167-180.

20. William Lanouette with Bela Szilard, *Genius in the Shadows*, pp. 183-184.

21. Joseph Rotblat, 'Societal Verification,' in *A Nuclear-Weapon-Free World ...*, ed. Rotblat, Steinberger and Udgaonkar, pp. 103-118.

22. See this volume, chapter 15.

23. See, for example, the argument to this effect in the 1997 testimony of Richard Perle, *op. cit.*

24. Committee on International Security and Arms Control, *The Future of U.S. Nuclear Weapons Policy*, p. 18.

25. *Ibid.*, pp. 82-83

26. *Ibid.*, p. 82

27. *Ibid.*, p. 15.

28. *Report of the Canberra Commission*, pp. 37-38.

29. Committee on International Security and Arms Control, *The Future of U.S. Nuclear Wapons Policy*, pp. 74-75.

30. *Ibid.*, p. 88.

31. Jonathan Schell, *The Abolition*

32. Committee on International Security and Arms Control, *The Future of U.S. Nuclear Weapons Policy*, p. 68.

33. *Ibid.*, p. 97.

34. Francesco Calogero, 'An Asymptotic Approach to a NWFW'

35. Andrew J. Goodpaster, Chair, Project on Eliminating Weapons of Mass Destruction, 'An Evolving U.S. Nuclear Posture,' Henry L. Stimson Center, Washington D.C., December 1995; Andrew J. Goodpaster, Chair, Project on Eliminating Weapons of Mass Destruction, 'An American Legacy: Building a Nuclear-Weapon-Free World,' Henry L. Stimson Center, Washington D.C., March 1997.

36. John P. Holdren, 'Thoughts on Science, Technology, and Human Well-Being in the Next 50 Years,' *APS News*, 7:4, April 1998, p. 12.

37. Natural Resources Defense Council, 'Table of Global Nuclear Stockpiles, 1945-1996,' available on the NRDC website at http://www.nrdc.org/nrdcpro/nudb/datab19.html.

6

Disinventing Nuclear Weapons

Francesco Calogero

The statement that 'nuclear weapons cannot be disinvented' is often put forward to argue for the infeasibility and/or the undesirability of a transition to a nuclear-weapon-free world. To assess the validity of this line of reasoning it is appropriate to investigate the actual meaning of the statement that 'nuclear weapons cannot be disinvented.'[1]

The knowledge that the laws of physics allow the construction of nuclear explosive devices cannot be forgotten. Moreover, especially as long as nuclear energy is routinely transformed into electrical energy by many utilities in many countries, a large body of nuclear engineering knowledge and expertise as well as large quantities of special nuclear materials – both of which would substantially ease any project aimed at constructing nuclear weapons – will continue to be available. And a considerable body of knowledge directly relevant to the construction of nuclear weapons is also accessible in the open literature; its disappearance is therefore impossible. Hence, the statement that 'nuclear weapons cannot be disinvented' is, at least to some degree, undoubtedly correct.

But there also exists a large additional body of knowledge, specifically focused on the construction of nuclear weaponry, which is classified and is therefore only known to relatively few people. The possibility that a little or a lot of this knowledge could disappear – by deliberate choice or by default – cannot be ruled out. There is indeed at least one case in which this has happened by choice. When the political leadership in South Africa decided to eliminate its secret nuclear weapons programme, not only was the nuclear arsenal (consisting of six operational warheads) dismantled and the resulting highly-enriched uranium (HEU) transferred to the civilian programme and put under international safeguards, but all the documentation (data, blueprints, *etc.*) relevant to the construction of nuclear weapons was deliberately eliminated.[2] And, to some extent, a loss of such relevant knowledge – due to the disappearance of individuals rather than the deliberate destruction of documentation – seems also to have happened by default in some other instances. For example, in certain countries the nuclear weapons option was actively pursued, at least at the research level, for a number of years and then abandoned (such as in Sweden, where a number of experts have since died).[3] Much additional progress in the direction of 'disinvention' could still be achieved in Sweden by eliminating existing libraries of classified reports.[4] So, in this limited sense, some progress towards 'disinventing nuclear weapons' can indeed occur.

There are two main ways in which classified knowledge is stored and preserved: (i) in written reports, computer codes, engineering blueprints, and physical objects which might serve as prototypes to be copied or reverse engineered; and (ii) as tacit knowledge, embodied in people rather than words, equations, or diagrams.[5] If a decision were made – within a specific environment – deliberately to eliminate this knowledge, it would clearly be easier to get rid quickly of that of type (i) than that of type (ii). The South African example demonstrates this obvious fact. On the other hand, if instead the goal is to preserve this knowledge in the context of a general end to nuclear weapons research and development, it might be more difficult to preserve the knowledge of type (ii) than that of type (i), at least over a time scale of many decades or centuries.

The secrecy that characterizes research on nuclear weapons is a clear indication that the possession and protection of this additional body of knowledge is considered quite important. It is, however, likely to be more relevant to the realization of advanced nuclear explosive devices than primitive ones. Hence the eventual disappearance of a little or a lot of this body of additional knowledge is probably of secondary importance in decreasing the risk of nuclear weapon proliferation – and in particular, the risk that subnational groups manufacture a presumably rather primitive nuclear explosive device for terrorist or criminal purposes.

The overriding argument implying that – if our civilization is to survive – an eventual transition to a nuclear-weapon-free world (NWFW) must occur, is the obvious fact that the present non-proliferation regime can only provide a temporary respite. It is inconceivable, in the long run, that only five states be allowed to possess nuclear weapons. The long-term solutions are either unchecked nuclear weapon proliferation, entailing inevitably the end of our civilization and perhaps of *Homo sapiens*, or the establishment of a NWFW.

Hence the question we realistically face is not whether a NWFW will be realized but when will it emerge, and how should we cope with the dangers that exist before a NWFW is established, as well as with the risks that linger in such a new regime, including in particular those associated with the difficulty of disinventing nuclear weapons.

A crucial question regarding the emergence of a NWFW is the time scale that is likely to characterize this inevitable transition. When is it likely to happen? How long will it take to complete the process?[6]

It is of course impossible to provide precise answers to these questions. Yet, barring exceptional events which might greatly accelerate the process, it is easy to advance plausible estimates. The entire history of nuclear weaponry spans half a century. The technological transformation of our civilization has an analogous, indeed perhaps somewhat shorter (and decreasing), time scale: half a century ago television did not exist, a quarter century ago there were no personal computers, ten years ago there were no portable telephones. The political, economic, industrial and technological transformation of Europe and Japan over the last half century has been extraordinary. That epochal transformation of our world, which goes under the name of 'the end of the Cold War' and includes the disappearance of the Soviet Union as well as the renunciation of nuclear weapons by four countries that had them (South Africa, Belarus, Kazakhstan, Ukraine), has taken less than one decade. From a technical point of view all existing nuclear weapons could be safely dismantled in a decade.

It appears, therefore, reasonable to estimate that the time unit to pace the transition to a NWFW is the decade, and that the transition is likely to take few such units. To the extent that one may plan for the future, it seems reasonable to assume that a NWFW will be in place half a century hence.

We are therefore thinking of developments likely to affect the life of our children and grandchildren – not only future generations far down the line.

Hence a question acquires particular relevance: Is there anything we could or should do now in the face of this prospect? And specifically – given the focus of this paper: Is there anything that might be done now to address the risks associated with the difficulty of disinventing nuclear weapons?

A serious risk that is already with us and will continue to exist in a NWFW is the possibility that a subnational group manufacture a nuclear explosive device, acquiring thereby the potential to destroy a city with all its inhabitants. There are two ways to try to prevent this happening. The first barrier is to stop such groups from getting hold of the raw materials that are needed to manufacture a nuclear explosive device. The essential ones are the fissile materials: especially highly-enriched uranium and plutonium. Of course in a NWFW – as well as now – an elaborate system of safeguards will be in place to verify that all such materials are accounted for and well protected. It will be essential to devote much care and adequate resources to this task. But unfortunately confidence would be unjustified in the complete effectiveness of such measures over several decades, especially concerning small leakages of material sufficient to manufacture just one nuclear explosive device, which is the typical option relevant to the subnational proliferation threat. Indeed only, say, four to eight kilograms of plutonium (or even less, depending on the sophistication of the implosion design) or from twenty (or even less, for an implosion device) to sixty (for a gun-configured device) kilograms of HEU are needed for a rather primitive nuclear explosive device (*e.g.* the Hiroshima bomb, which used 60 kilograms of 80% enriched uranium, or the South African bombs, which used 50 kilograms of 90% enriched uranium). The quantities of these materials that are now around, and that will continue to be around for the next few decades, are larger by at least five orders of magnitude, that is, the quantities of fissile materials available now are sufficient to manufacture well over *one hundred thousand* nuclear explosive devices. The quantities sufficient to build one, as mentioned above, can be hand-carried by a single individual in a suitcase, or perhaps two, for better walking balance, as well as to avoid criticality problems.

The second barrier is the difficulty in getting access to the technical competence required to manufacture a nuclear explosive device that has a significant chance of producing a substantial yield. This need not reach the multikiloton range to produce devastating effects. The basic knowledge needed to build such a device is widely available, but there can be little doubt that the task would be much easier for someone who has had previous experience of manufacturing nuclear weaponry than for somebody who lacks such training and specific knowledge.

It is therefore reasonable to anticipate that, in the context of a NWFW, the availability of large numbers of individuals knowledgeable about nuclear weapons technology would constitute a significant risk – the most acute embodiment, as it were, of the risk associated with the difficulty of disinventing nuclear weapons. Moreover, most such individuals would naturally be unemployed, hence they would constitute a burden for society, which should take care of their welfare. It would be dangerous to let them become too disgruntled! Some sort of surveillance of their whereabouts and activities would also be necessary, making them second-class citizens, since their very professional competence would constitute a potential risk.

In fact this problem is to a considerable extent now with us, especially in connection with the substantial (and to some degree catastrophic) downsizing of the nuclear weapons complex of the former Soviet Union. Considerable resources are needed to cope with it: more than US$1bn has been spent by the United States and other countries in trying to deal with this situation. A considerable fraction of these funds are specifically allocated to lessening the risks arising from the availability of too many individuals competent in nuclear weaponry. The main purpose of this essay is to focus attention on this aspect of the difficulty of disinventing nuclear weapons, in the context of the eventual realization of a NWFW which, for the reasons indicated above, I consider inevitable.

It is clear that the existence of many individuals with professional expertise in the manufacture of nuclear weapons will, in the circumstances of a NWFW, constitute a problem. The existence of a few such individuals in the initial phases of a NWFW might instead be expedient. This is because they might play a useful role in the monitoring of the regime and in building confidence in its viability and stability. Moreover, in the dismantling phase, such a presence is inevitable, since nuclear weapons experts will certainly be about as long as nuclear weapons exist, if only to take care of their dismantlement. Ultimately, however, the complete disappearance everywhere of all those who had a professional experience in designing, manufacturing and dismantling nuclear weapons will be a natural and permanent feature of a NWFW, as well, of course, as the eventual elimination of all blueprints, manuals, and so on.

It needs little reflection on the likely time scales of these processes, as compared with current life expectancies in our societies, to realize that many difficulties would be avoided if the cadre of experts on nuclear weaponry present at the time that a NWFW comes into being does not include young people. I submit that the time to begin addressing this problem is now.

While I have suggested that it might take a few decades to realize a NWFW, the possibility that this period be drastically reduced should not be ignored. This is likely to happen in the aftermath of a nuclear catastrophe, such as, for instance, an accident involving nuclear weapons or a nuclear explosion caused by a subnational group. Unfortunately, the possibility that some such event occur soon cannot be excluded; I think its likelihood is much higher than generally believed. In any case, prudent statesmanship should prepare for such an eventuality, if this can be done without significant collateral disadvantages.

The above considerations suggest that it would be politic to refrain henceforth from involving young people in research and development activities on nuclear weaponry. This could be easily realized by introducing, in all countries where such work is still in progress, a minimum age requirement for granting the security clearance necessary for such work. A little reflection on all the time scales involved, and on the potential efficacy of such an initiative, suggests setting such a minimum age at fifty; although it might make sense to introduce this rule gradually, aiming, say, at guaranteeing that one or two decades hence nobody under fifty has practical knowledge about the manufacture of nuclear weapons.

Note that such a decision would not now entail any drastic limitation on research and development activities on nuclear weaponry. It would be consistent with the commitment implied in the spirit of the Non-Proliferation Treaty and the Comprehensive Test Ban Treaty to proceed towards nuclear disarmament. Let me emphasize that under international law this is a binding obligation on all nuclear weapon states.[7]

It would also be consistent with common sense, which suggests a restrictive policy in the availability of know-how the use of which might have catastrophic consequences.

The institution by the nuclear weapon states of this policy would also send a clear message that their leadership takes seriously the commitment to proceed towards complete nuclear disarmament. I believe such a signal would make a useful – perhaps essential – conribution to sustaining the existing nuclear weapon non-proliferation regime, whose continued viability is very much in the interest of the nuclear weapon states, as well as the rest of the world. But this is, in my opinion, a secondary benefit. The main motivation for instituting such a policy is the security considerations outlined above.

It has been suggested to me[8] that the type of age restrictions in the recruitment of nuclear weaponeers advocated above will hardly be relevant once the notion becomes widespread that the technology of nuclear weaponry has no future, since no gifted young technologist will choose such an unpromising career. But this objection tends to ignore the reality of a job market which often does force people to choose work options because they are the only ones available, even if they are not the most palatable or auspicious. And it is indeed well known that, for instance in the United States, the nuclear weapons laboratories are still lavishly funded – in fact, paradoxically, even more so now than when the nuclear arms race was in full swing. This is because the laboratories had to be bribed to secure their acceptance of the CTBT – an acceptance that is considered essential to get the CTBT ratified by the US Senate.

It is to be expected that any suggestion along these lines will arouse – as I have personally experienced [9] – strong opposition from many nuclear weaponeers and in the nuclear weapons complexes. The reason is that it runs counter to a culture that puts a premium on continuing to push ahead with nuclear weapons research and development. However, one should never discount the chance that a good new idea could convince the most unlikely people.

But, perhaps more realistically, I believe the prospects for positive developments in this direction depend on pressure coming from civil society. This should eventually force, via the democratic process, interventions from the political leadership. That leadership should keep in mind, even now, before such pressure has built up, the possibility that some catastrophic event involving nuclear weaponry might suddenly cause a drastic change of mind in public opinion. Leaders might then have to explain why certain prudent moves were not undertaken when they might easily have been.

Nuclear weapons cannot be altogether disinvented; and this puts in question the viability of a NWFW, hence the future of our civilization. This problem is not insurmountable, as discussed elsewhere.[10] Moreover, something can be done to lessen – if not altogether to eliminate – it, as discussed above.

Clearly the first (rhetorical) question to be asked of someone who argues that the impossibility of disinventing nuclear weapons excludes the possibility of ever realizing a NWFW is: What then is the alternative long-term prospect for humankind? A free market for nuclear weapons so that every good citizen can have one? Another good question to then ask is: Why not try to do something – beginning now – to alleviate this problem?

Notes and References

1. It is a pleasure to acknowledge useful feedback on preliminary drafts of this paper from various colleagues, including in particular Steve Fetter, Tor Larsson and Pief Panofsky. The responsibility for all opinions and suggestions expressed herein are of course exclusively my own.
2. Waldo Stumpf, Birth and Death of the South African Nuclear Weapon Programme, in *Fifty Years of Nuclear Weapons,* Proceedings of the Sixth Castiglioncello Conference, USPID, 1996. See also by the same author: South Africa's Nuclear Weapons Programme: From Deterrence to Dismantlement, *Arms Control Today,* December 1995/January 1996, pp. 3-8; David Fischer, Reversing Nuclear Proliferation: South Africa, *Security Dialogue,* 24, pp. 273-286, 1993.
3. Tor Larsson, 'The Swedish Nuclear and Non-Nuclear Postures,' forthcoming.
4. Tor Larsson, private communication.
5. Donald MacKenzie and Graham Spinardi, Tacit Knowledge, Weapons Design, and the Uninvention of Nuclear Weapons, *Amer. J. Sociology,* 101, pp. 44-49, July 1995.
6. Let me emphasize that I do not discuss here any detail of how to achieve a NWFW, of its overall viability, nor indeed what the notion of a NWFW precisely means. For analysis on these points see, for example, *A Nuclear-*

Weapon-Free   World: Desirable?   Feasible?,   ed.   Joseph Rotblat, Jack Steinberger and Bhalchandra Udgaonkar, Boulder, Co.: Westview Press, 1993.

7.   'There exists an obligation to pursue in good faith and bring to a conclusion negotiations leading to nuclear disarmament in all its aspects under strict and effective international control.' Unanimous part of the *Advisory Opinion on the Legality of the Threat or Use of Nuclear Weapons* issued on July 8, 1996, by the International Court of Justice in The Hague.

8.   Tor Larsson, private communication.

9.   Interventions from various participants in the Pugwash workshop on nuclear forces which took place at the nuclear weapon laboratory *Chelyabinsk-70* in Snezhinsk, Russia, September 1997.

10. See *A Nuclear-Weapon-Free World: Desirable? Feasible?*, ed. Joseph Rotblat, Jack Steinberger and Bhalchandra Udgaonkar; and other chapters in *The Force of Reason*.

7

Scientists and the Abolition of Nuclear Weapons

Iwao Ogawa

Ever since the tragedies of Hiroshima and Nagasaki, all humanity, and particularly the Japanese, have sought to achieve the abolition of nuclear weapons. This is at last becoming a realizable and realistic aim after several recent international accords. They include the indefinite extension of the Nuclear Non-Proliferation Treaty; the conclusion of the Comprehensive Test Ban Treaty (CTBT), prohibiting unconditionally all nuclear test explosions; and the Advisory Opinion of the International Court of Justice, calling nuclear weapons the ultimate evil, although not deciding upon the legality of their use or threat of use in self-defence.

In this atmosphere, several authoritative groups, national and international, have made proposals for further nuclear disarmament aiming for the complete elimination of nuclear weapons. These proposals are contained in publications from the Pugwash Conferences, the Henry L. Stimson Center, the US National Academy of Sciences, and the Canberra Commission. In addition, a variety of draft conventions for the prohibition of nuclear weapons have been formulated by groups of lawyers and by NGOs.

All these documents deserve careful study and appreciation, since they have succeeded in reviewing the wide range of measures and steps to be taken and have arranged them in a feasible order. However, a radical change in the thinking of the nuclear weapon states will be needed before they make a political decision to accept such measures. There will also need to be a transformation of the principles of national security, as emphasized in the Russell-Einstein Manifesto of 1955.

The main obstacle to nuclear disarmament is the strategy of nuclear deterrence, which regards the nuclear weapon as a necessary evil indispensable to national security. It should be noted that there exists in the background in the nuclear weapon states a strong national belief in military force and political pressure from the military-industrial complex. The latter has long received huge benefits from the strategy of nuclear deterrence.

As is well known, the doctrine of deterrence rests on the idea of preventing a possible attack or invasion by threatening nuclear retaliation. This is entirely contrary to natural humanity based on mutual confidence and constitutes a quite out-of-place and wild barbarism.

It should be remembered here that the nuclear weapon was born originally during the Second World War from the fear felt by scientists about the possible acquisition of an atomic bomb by Nazi Germany. The following arms race between East and West during the Cold War was also a result of fear felt by both camps about the possible build-up of arsenals on the other side.

In military strategy, the roles of nuclear weapons are always considered only from the point of view of their large explosive yield and destructive power, with little concern for their inhumane consequences. Their deployment or use is generally made under some justification such as national defence, or to deter a nuclear attack by another country. Here the inhumanity and immorality inherent in nuclear weapons are taken as a necessary evil that must be accepted for the declared purpose.

The unprecedented disasters of Hiroshima and Nagasaki, and the serious radiation diseases and subsequent deaths suffered by the fishermen on board the Lucky Dragon V and the inhabitants of nearby islands, caused by a US H-bomb test conducted at the Bikini Atoll in 1954, have simply been regarded, respectively, as a 'means to reduce the number of losses to the Allied Force in wartime' and 'unfortunate victims in the way of defence activity in the Cold War.' No formal apology nor compensation have been made thus far for either event.

In this way, nuclear weapon states continue to adhere throughout to the posture of considering nuclear weapons as a necessary wrong to be retained indefinitely. Thus they succeeded in influencing the International Court of Justice to avoid judgement in its Advisory Opinion as to whether the threat or use of nuclear weapons is lawful or unlawful 'in an extreme circumstance of self-defence, in which the very survival of a State would be at stake.'

The policy 'not to use or threaten to use nuclear weapons unless there is a just cause,' or more briefly 'not to use nukes if not necessary,' reminds me of an exquisite joke by the late Leo Szilard, who had a fine sense of irony, namely a set of maxims entitled *Zehn Gebote* (Ten Commandments): *'Lüge nicht ohne Notwendigkeit'* (Do not lie without need). In short, the statement implies 'to use if necessary' and may even be rewritten as 'if nukes were used, then there was a need.' By repeating such a tautology in respect to their nuclear policy, the nuclear weapon states have lost completely the confidence and respect of the majority of peoples of the world. The only correct recognition of nuclear weapons today must be none other than an absolute evil that must never be used in any case – as asserted by the late Professor Hideki Yukawa.

During the Cold War, when the East and West continued a seemingly endless arms race, maintenance of nuclear arsenals and the strategy of nuclear deterrence might have had an apparent rationality. After the collapse of the Soviet Union, however, any military importance or political role for nuclear weapons almost completely disappeared, from the standpoint of the nuclear powers. There are no longer any hostile confrontations between them, so that the term 'nuclear deterrence' has become obsolete and meaningless. No scenario exists in which the threat or use of nuclear weapons deserves serious consideration. In fact, many ex-generals and ex-admirals have recently joined in a statement pointing out the absence of military value of nuclear weapons and supporting action towards their abolition.

Despite such a state of affairs, the US Department of Energy (DOE) is promoting a large scale weapons-related project named the Stockpile Stewardship and Management Program. In the name of fundamental research, most of the programme budget is directed at the construction or reconstruction of gigantic facilities, presumably based on the ideas of experts belonging to weapons research laboratories or to weapons industries.

While the military value of nuclear weapons seems certainly to be decreasing rapidly, all the nuclear weapon states insist on holding their nuclear arsenals indefinitely and continue efforts to strengthen and improve them. Whatever military purpose they may cite, the driving force behind this policy is the desperate manoeuvring of military industries, weapons engineers, related bureaucrats, politicians, and the like, to defend their enormous vested interests, having lost their *raison d'être* after the end of Cold War.

The efforts of any groups or individuals towards a nuclear-weapon-free-world should not, therefore, be aimed only at some particular international agreements: for example, reduction of certain weapons, prohibition of production, tests and deployment of these weapons, prevention of their proliferation, prohibition of nuclear first strike and nuclear attack against non-nuclear weapon states, and so on, but also at the vested interests mentioned above.

Any kind of basic research and development for military purposes should be rejected as contrary to disarmament and as a wasteful folly impairing the welfare, environment and culture of the nation. It should be one of the important social responsibilities of scientists to perceive immediately such research and development, to examine its intention and contents, and to warn the government and the public of its undesirability and draw attention to associated problems.

More radically, however, the most serious but difficult task or mission imposed on scientists should be to help people all over the world to recognize the nuclear weapon as an outright evil and reconfirm the present-day significance of the final appeal in the Russell-Einstein Manifesto – 'Remember your humanity, and forget the rest' – in solving any international issue.

There are still many people in the world, even in Japan, who do not know well the reality of the disasters in Hiroshima and Nagasaki nor the potential threat of the huge nuclear stockpiles held by the big powers. In order to achieve a radical increase in awareness, tremendous efforts must be made to attract attention to the matter. It will help greatly if as much information and as many opportunities as possible are provided for learning these serious facts. Scientists have much to do in assisting these onerous endeavours.

One of the difficult problems is how those scientists or engineers who are working in weapons industries or laboratories can fulfil their social responsibility to work towards a nuclear-weapon-free world. It will not always be easy for them to join external social activities. However, as specialists they know the matter best and may have valuable opinions. External scientists should try to communicate with them as fully as possible. In case any ominous sign should appear suggesting the onset of a dangerous arms race or research and development of provocative new weapons, these scientists must conscientiously observe the progress that is made and warn the public at the earliest opportunity.

In a historical period in which an epoch-making effort of mankind to eliminate and abolish nuclear weapons is beginning to bear fruit, scientists must recognize their unique role and special responsibility to contribute to its final success.

Motives for individual scientists to become conscious of their social responsibility may differ. In the case of the author, the strongest motive was the extraordinary experience of looking up at the mushroom cloud of the first atomic bomb dropped on Hiroshima. At that time, I was twenty-three years of age and working about sixteen kilometres to the south of the centre of Hiroshima city, at the Naval College as a technical officer teaching mechanics to students.

On the fine morning of the August 6, 1945, I was organizing a group of students on the campus who were building a soil shelter for trucks and standing on its top facing towards the south. Several minutes after an air-raid warning was cancelled, I was suddenly irradiated by an intense flash of light from the north. After more than half a minute, a strong blast followed. On hearing a later warning siren, I led the students to shelter in a cave, looking up on the way at the rapidly growing head of a bright cloud similar to a cumulo-cirrus. Coming back to the quarters later, I was surprised to find that many window-panes and roof-bricks had fallen to the ground and were scattered around.

From the many observations and findings from the strenuous investigation of the ruins carried out by my colleagues of various disciplines a few days after the bombing, it was soon confidently concluded that the bomb was nuclear. As a young physicist who was dreaming of joining research in pure nuclear physics, I was greatly shocked by the fact that the brilliant achievements of nuclear physics had produced a terrible means of unprecedented destruction and indiscriminate massacre. As the only nuclear physicist who saw, from the ground, the mushroom cloud above Hiroshima, I could not help resolving to do my best to support the worldwide movement against the nuclear arms race and to talk to the public about the threat of global radioactive fallout from nuclear explosions.

It was in connection with my opposition to nuclear weapons that I was asked by Professors Yukawa and Tomonaga to help them at the First Pugwash Conference in 1957. This historical conference, which was held in response to the call of the Russell-Einstein Manifesto, was of great significance. It was not only the first opportunity for scientists, including those from East and West, to meet together to discuss international affairs such as nuclear disarmament, but also a valuable workshop for scientific assessment of the danger arising from the advent of thermonuclear weapons. It was an unexpected honour and pleasure for me to attend such an important meeting. It was at this meeting that I was privileged to become acquainted with Professor Rotblat, one of the main organizers of the Conference. From the first, I was strongly attracted to his pertinent and thoughtful initiatives in the discussion, as well as to his warm and kind personality. During the ensuing forty years, I have always respected him and learned much from him about the Pugwash movement and scientific matters, especially about the biological effects of nuclear radiation. The most important lesson I owe him, however, arises from his lifelong and self-sacrificing efforts, as a nuclear physicist, towards a nuclear-weapon-free world.

8

Of Men, their Minds and the Bomb

Jasjit Singh

'War is waged by men, not by beasts, nor by gods'

A knife is a knife ... is a knife. It has been used for centuries for a multiplicity of tasks. A knife is used at times of joy and celebrations. The Christmas cake, the wedding cake, the birthday cake of a child or his grandfather, and religious ceremonies, in most cases all require a knife. The surgeon has always used it in his profession of healing and saving life. The knife has also been used for centuries to take life. The killing with a knife itself has been undertaken often for a criminal purpose, whether premeditated or otherwise. The knife has also provided the choice to kill in self-defence. Many other variations could be cited.

The knife cannot be 'disinvented.' When other men go about carrying knives with the expressly stated purpose of using them, and using them first, and to kill, others feel the compulsion to acquire the knife for their own safety and security. The spread of knives cannot be controlled. So how should the problem of knives be addressed?

The answer lies in the fact that the central issue is not the knife itself. Man killed man even in the Stone Age. The knife is but an instrument, a tool or a weapon in the hand of man. What decides whether the tool will be used as a weapon, for good or for evil, lies in the mind of the man wielding it, and the ideas and the belief systems behind the use, usability and legitimacy of that knife for killing or peaceful purposes.

Prohibiting the use of the knife for wanton or violent purposes, therefore, is by itself an important step to stop the crime or killings. But it cannot be achieved unless the ideas and beliefs in its utility and usability alter. It also requires that norms, inhibitions and legal regimes regulating the use of knives for peaceful purposes are established and enforced.

Unlike the knife, nuclear weapons do not have a dual use although nuclear science and technology has. Nuclear weapons are universally acknowledged as the most horrendous instrument of mass destruction, not discriminating between combatants and non-combatants, innocents or guilty. So, what are the reasons that nuclear weapons are sought after? The following questions and answers might provide some clarification:

What are the targets of nuclear weapons? Nuclear weapons.
What provocation could bring about the use of nuclear weapons? Nuclear weapons.
What is the defence against nuclear weapons? Nuclear weapons.
How do we prevent the use of nuclear weapons? By threatening to use nuclear weapons.
Why can't nuclear weapons be abolished? Nuclear weapons.[1]

To this can be added one more question: What is the strongest driving force of nuclear proliferation? Nuclear weapons!

There is near universal agreement that nuclear weapons must be abolished. Even countries such as the United States acknowledge that the elimination of nuclear weapons is a policy goal, even if undefined in time and method. But there is little movement and still less commitment towards such a goal. Some agreements for nuclear arms reduction have taken place, although the schedules are already slipping. Deeper reductions may be expected in the coming decade, but not a firm commitment to disarmament let alone concrete progress. A Comprehensive Test Ban Treaty has been signed but is unable to enter-into-force except possibly provisionally among the signatories under some tenuous arrangements. Further progress on non-proliferation measures is also blocked by the big gap between positions seeking abolition of nuclear weapons on one side and merely to strengthen non-proliferation on the other.

The world has reached a momentous point in its history where the role of nuclear weapons in the twenty-first century needs to be redefined. And yet there is strong resistance to do so on any rational basis or on grounds of humanity.

In 1993, four years after the end of Cold War, the CSIS Nuclear Strategy Study Group (in the USA) lamented that

it would be a tragedy if the present momentum toward international co-operation and disarmament passed without some attempt to establish a more robust nuclear end-state whose practical effect is virtually to eliminate the risk that nuclear weapons will be used.[2]

The permanent extension of the Non-Proliferation Treaty (NPT) in May

1995 without any unambiguous, let alone binding, commitment to nuclear disarmament only reinforced the concerns held that nuclear disarmament is not likely to be pursued by the weapon states in any meaningful way in the foreseeable future.

The risks of proliferation, which were markedly enhanced consequent to the break up of the Soviet Union, are likely to continue well into the next century. Illicit trafficking in fissile material has been a cause of serious concern now for a number of years. More recently, claims by those previously in authority reveal that portable 'suitcase bombs' are not fully accounted for in Russia. There have been reports of clandestine transfer of nuclear weapons from the former Soviet Union. China has helped Pakistan acquire nuclear weapons by supplying nuclear weapons technology and materials (including ballistic missiles) in gross violation of its commitments to regimes such as the NPT. Action against violations of non-proliferation norms by the five permanent members of the UN Security Council will remain extremely problematic.

While the risks of a large scale nuclear war may have receded somewhat after the end of the Cold War, the dangers emanating from nuclear weapons are being carried forward into the twenty-first century. The indefinite extension of the NPT has legitimized the possession of nuclear weapons in perpetuity, even if only in the hands of five countries. Even the existing nuclear arms control agreements (such as START II) are not being implemented according to the original promises. Whatever momentum for nuclear disarmament existed earlier, which was precious little in itself, has been largely replaced by enhanced emphasis on non-proliferation and counter-proliferation. The industrialized developed countries, who, technically speaking, may be non-nuclear weapon states, but rely politically on nuclear weapons through alliances, are equally responsible for perpetuating nuclear weapons and diverting attention from disarmament.

Some new voices have also emerged in the post-Cold War world to join the international community in demanding total elimination of nuclear weapons. China, unlike Russia, still supports the elimination of nuclear weapons, and has been seeking a no-first-use treaty among the weapon states. In the report of a committee chaired by General Andrew Goodpaster, competent people, including a former US defence secretary and senior military commanders, have argued that US security will be enhanced with total elimination of nuclear weapons.[3] They have recommended a phased programme of disarmament that could be achieved in a couple of decades. Cold War theologians such as Paul Nitze, Fred Iklé and very senior military commanders who till recently were in command of the US nuclear arsenal (for example, General Lee Butler, who headed the US

Strategic Command until 1994) have seriously questioned the wisdom of retaining nuclear weapons. The Australian Prime Minister, Paul Keating, when announcing the setting up of the Canberra Commission of experts to work out a plan for total elimination of nuclear weapons stated that, 'I believe that a world free of nuclear weapons is now feasible.'[4] He went on to say that, 'We want the nuclear weapons states to carry out their commitments to the elimination of their nuclear stockpiles by adopting a systematic process to achieve that result.' The G-21 resolution in the CD specifically seeks tangible progress on nuclear disarmament.

The adoption of the resolution on Principles and Objectives during the NPT extension conference itself reaffirms the commitment contained in Article VI of the NPT to negotiate the complete elimination of nuclear weapons. Modern civilization prides itself on the belief that rule of law guides its existence and functioning. Rule of law is claimed to be the foundation of civil society. The World Court, responding to a request from the UN General Assembly, ruled unanimously in July 1996 that 'There exists an obligation to pursue in good faith and bring to a conclusion negotiations leading to nuclear disarmament in all aspects under strict international control.'[5] Yet this seems to have been ignored by the five weapon states.

Countries such as India are likely to continue exerting maximum pressure for total abolition of nuclear weapons. But it is also clear that at the root of the resistance to abolition are the beliefs held about the use and usability of nuclear weapons. Change to the ideas and beliefs used to justify nuclear weapons is a vital ingredient in moving towards total abolition of nuclear weapons.

An abiding lesson of human civilization is that all significant changes in history have been brought about by the force of ideas. Changes in how we approach an issue, and the ideas prevalent among people at large, and the decision-makers in particular, create the conditions for change. Attitudes and beliefs play a crucial role in shaping policies. The lesson of the Indian struggle for freedom is perhaps instructive. India's independence, fifty years ago, was not won through a violent conflict but through a non-violent struggle which relied on influencing the way people thought about colonial rule and independence. Mahatma Gandhi mobilized public opinion to convince the Imperial ruling power that continued colonial rule was no longer a viable option. The force of ideas led not only to India's independence but also initiated the dismantlement of colonial empires world-wide. Similarly, apartheid was finally deconstructed because the belief that it could be sustained indefinitely changed. A decade ago, this was not considered possible by most analysts. The Cold War ended due to the force of ideas opening up a closed dogmatic authoritarian system. Earlier, strong resistance to abolishing slavery finally broke down in the face of the force of ideas, being no longer supportable or tolerable in the emerging liberal, civilized society. Human history has repeatedly proved that what was unthinkable can soon become the norm once a belief system alters.

When a young Joseph Rotblat walked out of the Manhattan Project and away from building nuclear weapons it was because of his belief and ideas.

Is the present situation conducive to a change in the ideas about the use and usability of nuclear weapons, so as to make them redundant? Objectively, the answer is 'yes,' although substantive steps will have to be taken to establish norms and a legal framework to sustain a nuclear-weapon-free world. Three arguments can be made in support of this argument.

Firstly, there are new voices demanding that nuclear weapons be abolished. Unlike the majority of the peace movement in the 1980s, the people who are asserting that nuclear weapons lack utility include persons who till recently were heading the nuclear forces of superpowers, prepared to launch global destruction on a single command.

Secondly, the most likely scenario for actual use of nuclear weapons is believed to be associated with a conventional war, but the probability of such war has been receding over the decades. While some people may argue that this is because of the existence of nuclear weapons, the reality is that modern (developed and developing) states are becoming increasingly vulnerable to the consequences of even a conventional war. Use of conventional high explosives in Europe could lead to hundreds of Chernobyls overnight. Millions of tonnes of chemicals are in transit in Europe at any time; extensive, almost unacceptable damage and casualties, would arise as a consequence of conventional attacks on these. Territorial wars are no longer viable for a variety of reasons. Rapid communications, political awareness, and social changes have ensured that populations cannot be held under control against their wish. Increasing globalization of economy and trade bind the world into a situation where a war will adversely affect everyone. A reduction in defence spending world-wide since 1988 of more than a third, retrenchment of military power, and acute problems of resupply of weapons and equipment, have made war an extremely costly endeavour even for developed industrial countries. It is often forgotten that even the powerful USA was able to put together a coalition of forces and conduct the Gulf War in 1990-91 only with massive financial support from other countries such as Japan, Saudi Arabia and Germany. Conventional wisdom is fundamentally flawed when it argues that a major war between the major powers will be more likely in the absence of nuclear weapons. For these and many more reasons, regular inter-state war, of the traditional kind, is hardly likely to persist in the twenty-first century as a viable instrument of policy in the classical Clausewitzean sense. Thus, with war itself less likely in the coming decades, the utility of nuclear weapons is even more questionable.

Thirdly, what contribution can nuclear weapons make to the security of states? They serve no rational military purpose. They cannot deter terrorism. The only conceivable rational purpose that nuclear weapons can serve is to deter another country's nuclear weapons. But it will be cheaper and immensely less risky to eliminate the threat by abolishing nuclear weapons. Nuclear weapons do, on the other hand, provide a tremendously powerful political instrument of coercion.[6] This applies in situations of nuclear asymmetry. The end of the Cold War confrontation has brought clarity to the nuclear situation: nuclear weapons have a disproportionately high value as a political instrument of influence and coercion. The destructive power of the bomb has raised the political value of the bomb.

But the problem is that the propagation of a linear nuclear doctrinal theology, for more than fifty years, has numbed human consciousness about nuclear weapons. The USA had the bomb, so the Soviet Union needed it. And China needed it. The USA then needed more of them to deter the Soviet Union and China. In between the UK and France slipped into the equation. Doctrinal changes and changes in the ideas and attitudes towards nuclear weapons are essential if we are to reverse the trend and eliminate nuclear weapons, at least from national arsenals. And reversal is not progressing because generations have grown up in the nuclear weapon states (and the so-called non-nuclear weapon states, protected by nuclear weapons) believing that the bomb has preserved peace and hence harbouring a great reluctance to let it go.

Behind this line of thinking are deeper trends, especially those dealing with the increased legitimacy of targeting civil society. Society has always been involved in war preparedness and in contributing the means and manpower for wars. However, until the closing years of the eighteenth century, wars were less destructive, especially in relation to society.[7] War was exclusively the undertaking of armies and navies. Restraint was not only a characteristic of eighteenth century battles and strategy. The attitudes towards the civilian population had changed notably after the large-scale casualties of the Thirty Years War. Military planners and commanders made serious efforts to preserve society from the ravages of war. Pre-French Revolution assessments were that: 'At the present day war is carried on by regular armies; the people, the peasantry, the townsfolk take no part in it and as a rule have nothing to fear from the sword of the enemy.'[8] Frederick the Great, in fact, even believed that 'when engaged in war, the civilian population should not even be aware that a state of war existed.'[9] Developments arising out of the Industrial Revolution (leading to the industrialization of war) and the French Revolution (with its revolutionary nationalism) resulted in society itself becoming included in war and war-fighting. This also coincided with the beginning of the totality of war which finally culminated in the world wars of this century. The American Civil War reinforced the model of mass armies pitted against each other in years of battle, with the societies (of North and South) mobilized behind them.

At the beginning of the nineteenth century, especially during the Napoleonic Wars, mobilization of the nation for war had become an integral element in international security. At the same time, subjugation and destruction of the 'national will' had become one of the primary objectives of war and the application of military power. This brought society within the ambit of war and inter-state conflict. Targeting of the civilian population was increasingly seen as legitimate. Mobilization of the nation for war provided plentiful human resources, motivated by patriotic and ideological fervour. This provided the leadership with a margin of safety that the smaller professionalized military power was unable to provide. Progress in technology threatened to increase the ability to cause pain and punishment.

The First World War saw the total war model coming into its own with the emergence of the political economy of war on one side, and the expansion of military-technological means to bring society totally within the fold of war on the other. As Ludendorff was to write: 'The nature of totalitarian warfare literally demands the entire strength of the nation, since such a war is directed against it.'[10] Two developments were to further increase the inclusion of the population in war. The success of the Bolshevik Revolution in Russia established the foundations of not only a new revolutionary model, but also one where the 'export of revolutions' was an integral component of the ideology. Its further evolution was to be based on the use of violence (and repression); and most of the century was to pass by before the Russians altered the basic ideology. However, the model of the export of ideology still exists and has been pursued by other states and political entities.

The legitimacy of targeting civil society is at the root of the phenomenon where civilian casualties in military conflicts have been on the increase. The implication of society being made a prime target in warfare may be seen by the changing ratio of civil/military casualties in wars of this century noted in the table below:

| | Ratio of Casualties | |
	Civil	**Military**
First World War	1	20
Second World War	1	1
Korean War	5	1
Vietnam War	20	1

It may be argued that civilian casualties have been much lower in some of the later wars (like the Gulf War 1990-91). But the important point to note is that the targeting of population centres has continued. Iraq fired 86 Scud-type ballistic missiles, almost entirely against population centres in Israel and Saudi Arabia. This should be seen in the context of earlier threats by Iraq to use chemical weapons. The 'War of Cities' during the Iran-Iraq War (1980-88) involved over 600 ballistic missiles fired against city centres of either side. Missile attacks on Kabul have been a perennial phenomenon for nearly a decade. In fact, nearly 25,000 surface-to-surface missiles have been fired in wars in the last five decades. Barring a few dozen, all of them have targeted population centres, and have been perceived to succeed in their objective.

The second development concerned the extension of warfare through the advent of air power. Liberated from earlier limitations of having to necessarily destroy the adversary's military or conquer his territory first, air warfare made it possible to target the adversary nation's society directly. Early attempts to control the process failed. On the other hand, Western Europe and US strategists believed that air power would project the spear point of a nation's military force behind the frontline of the battlefield (and thus avoid the horrors and costs of trench warfare) into an enemy's vital areas to render it powerless to defend itself. Aerial bombing would cause such destruction and paralysis that 'resistance is no longer possible and capitulation is the outcome.'[11] The central target was the enemy nation.

Douhet was forthright about inflicting terror from the skies when he prophesied that victory 'must depend upon smashing the material and moral resources of a people caught in a frightful cataclysm which haunts them everywhere without cease till the final collapse of all social organization.'[12] As technology advanced and matured, this was manifested in the 'strategic' bombings of the Second World War, with the killings of people in the bombing of Dresden, the decimation of Coventry, the fire-bombing of Tokyo, and the final culmination at Hiroshima and Nagasaki. Society had become incorporated fully into the total war paradigm. Nuclear strategies, with the potential for mass destruction and nuclear winter, have perpetuated the pattern since then. Society needs to be rescued from the doctrines and ideas justifying these targeting practices.

Two parallel paths have to be followed in moving towards the abolition of nuclear weapons: the deep reduction of arsenals and their elimination from national control; and a process of changing the beliefs, attitudes and ideas supporting the use and usability of nuclear weapons. As we approach the end of the millennium, after what has been the most violent and destructive century in human history, we need to remember our humanity.

Unfortunately, even the arguments for reduction and elimination of nuclear arsenals do not address the 'software' problem of the minds of men which seek to justify the retention of nuclear weapons. The critical task is to challenge the nuclear belief system by addressing the minds of men who believe the bomb is a necessity and has a utility.

A major step in this process is the creation of legal and international norms against the use of nuclear weapons. In 1996 the World Court concluded that there is no specific law that makes nuclear weapons illegal, although their use would be generally inconsistent with rules of armed conflict and humanitarian laws. As long as there is no specific legal obstacle to the possession and use of nuclear weapons, states are likely to continue believing that such weapons are legitimate and acceptable to the international community. It is necessary, therefore, that an appropriate legal norm be established so that elimination of nuclear weapons can be expedited. This is best achieved through a convention to outlaw the use and threat of use of nuclear weapons.

The Geneva Convention established a legal norm against the use of chemical weapons in 1925. Although some states joined it a good half-century later, it operated as a strong inhibition against the use of chemical weapons, at least until 1988. It was the absence of any strong reaction against the violation of the Geneva Convention by Iraq that emboldened it to threaten extensive use of these weapons in 1990-91.

A resolution calling for the use and threat of use of nuclear weapons to be outlawed has been moved and passed by a majority vote at the UN General Assembly regularly since 1978. The interest of some of the key players that pressed for such a convention appears to have flagged somewhat. But if the goal of elimination of nuclear weapons is to be translated into reality, it will be necessary to establish the norms and legal framework that delegitimize such weapons.

The second area is related to doctrinal changes to reinforce the process of delegitimization. There is an urgent need for a binding political agreement among the eight nuclear weapon states (the five declared weapon states, plus India, Pakistan and Israel) not to be the first to use nuclear weapons. Of these, China and India have always supported the concept of a no-first-use pledge. The Soviet Union used to support the concept also, but the Russian Federation has moved away from that position. However, this is not an absolutist shift. In 1996 Russia and China agreed to a bilateral no-first-use (of nuclear weapons) commitment within a broader non-aggression pact. In a profound change from its earlier position, NATO adopted the position in July 1990 that nuclear weapons were 'truly weapons of last resort.' The new Strategic Concept adopted by NATO in November 1991 further relegated nuclear weapons to the margins of NATO strategy by stating that the circumstances in which any use of nuclear weapons might have to be contemplated are 'remote.'

The new NATO-Russia Founding Act signed in Paris on May 27, 1997, states that 'Russia and NATO do not see each other as adversaries.' President Clinton, speaking about the Charter stated that 'The veil of hostility between East and West has lifted. Together we see a future of partnership too long delayed that must no longer be denied.' President Chirac of France and Chancellor Kohl of Germany endorsed these views. As early as 1993, a seminal study by eminent experts in the USA had concluded that:

> The changing political landscape in Europe has produced a strategic revolution; neither deterrence of conventional attack nor deterrence of nuclear attack any longer requires the presence of large numbers of ... nuclear weapons on the European continent.[13]

In the view of many experts, the current NATO position is well short of a no-first-use commitment. But if more recent developments are any indication, there is no reason why the NATO states would/should not go to full commitment to no first use at an early date. The most important development is the recent agreement between NATO and Russia regarding NATO expansion where President Yeltsin made the surprise announcement that Russian nuclear weapons have been taken off their earlier mission of targeting NATO member countries.

Difficulties may also arise from Israel and Pakistan not coming forth with such commitments. In this case, the agreement could be concluded among the five declared nuclear weapon states and India, with Israel and Pakistan invited to join at the earliest opportunity.

In the ultimate analysis, change in the way we think about the bomb will support and even drive the thrust for abolition of nuclear weapons. For nuclear weapons to be abolished, it is equally, if not more, important to ensure that the bomb is regarded as an irrelevant factor in the day to day business of international politics. This can only take place if men change the way they think about the bomb. A no-first-use convention and a convention to outlaw the use and threat of use of nuclear weapons would go a long way in changing the minds of men who otherwise casually talk about hundreds if not thousands of nuclear weapons to be kept for use against humanity.

Notes and References

1. William Arkin, 'The Bomb has Many Friends,' *The Bulletin of Atomic Scientists,* March/April 1997, p. 37.
2. *Toward a Nuclear Peace: The Future of Nuclear Weapons in US Foreign and Defense Policy,* Report by the CSIS Nuclear Strategy Study Group, Washington D.C.: Centre for Strategic and International Studies, June 1993, p. 67.
3. *An Evolving US Nuclear Posture,* Second Report of the Steering Committee, Project on Eliminating Weapons of Mass Destruction, Henry L. Stimson Center, Washington DC, December 1995.
4. P.J. Keating, Prime Minister of Australia. Speech given on the 50th Anniversary of the United Nations, October 24, 1995.
5. *Legality of the Threat or Use of Nuclear Weapons,* Advisory Opinion, Communiqué No. 96/23, July 8, 1996, International Court of Justice, The Hague.
6. Even during the Cold War, the real effect of nuclear weapons was political, especially in a coercive role, since it was recognized early on that actual use would annihilate the human race itself. The coercive role was practised through treats of use.
7. Carl Von Clausewitz, *On War,* ed. Anatol Rapoport, Middlesex, UK: Penguin Books, 1968.
8. Vattel in *Laws of Nations,* cited by Sir Basil Liddell Hart, *The Sword and the Pen*, London: Book Club Associates, 1978, p. 85.
9. Geoffrey Treasure, *The Making of Modern Europe 1648-1780,* London: Metheum, 1985.
10. Erich Ludendorff in *The Nation at War,* cited by Liddell Hart in *The Sword and the Pen.*
11. W.F. Craven and J.B. Cate eds., *The Army Air Forces in World War II,* Chicago: University of Chicago Press, 1948.
12. Lee Kennett, *A History of Strategic Bombing,* New York: Charles Scriber, 1982.
13. *Toward a Nuclear Peace,* p. 28.

Ending War

9

Reflections on War in the Twenty-First Century

Robert S. McNamara

I want to begin by recounting my earliest memory as a child. It is of a city exploding with joy. The city was San Francisco. The date November 11, 1918 – Armistice Day. I was two years old. The city was celebrating not only the end of the First World War, but the belief, held so strongly by President Wilson, and by many other Americans, that the United States and its allies had won a war to end all wars.

They were wrong, of course. The twentieth century was on its way to becoming the bloodiest, by far, in all of human history: during it, 160 million people will have been killed in conflicts – within nations and between nations – across the globe. Were similar conflicts to take place in the twenty-first century, when population will have risen three fold and when wars are likely to be fought with weapons of mass destruction, fatalities would be substantially higher – at least 300 million.

Is that what we want in the first century of the new millennium? I hope not.

If not, the time to initiate action to prevent that tragedy is now.

We should begin by establishing a realistic appraisal of the problem. It is readily apparent, very complex and very dangerous.

The Carnegie Commission stated it very clearly when it said:

Peace – will require greater understanding and respect for differences within and across national boundaries. We humans do not have the luxury any longer of indulging our prejudices and ethnocentrism. They are anachronisms of our ancient past. The worldwide historical record is full of hateful and destructive behaviour based on religious, racial, political, ideological, and other distinctions – holy wars of one sort or another.

Will such behaviour in the next century be expressed with weapons of mass destruction? If we cannot learn to accommodate each other respectfully in the twenty-first century, we could destroy each other at such a rate that humanity will have little to cherish.[1]

The Commission is saying, in effect, that the end of the Cold War in 1989 did not, and will not, in and of itself, result in an end to conflict. We see evidence of the truth of that statement on all sides. The Iraqi invasion of Kuwait, the civil war in the former Yugoslavia, the turmoil in Northern Iraq, the tension between India and Pakistan, the unstable relations between North and South Korea, and the conflicts across the face of sub-Saharan Africa in Somalia, Sudan, Rwanda, Burundi, Zaire, Sierra Leone and Liberia. These all make clear that the world of the future will not be without conflict, conflict between disparate groups within nations and conflict extending across national borders. Racial, religious and ethnic tensions will remain. Nationalism will be a powerful force across the globe. Political revolutions will erupt as societies advance. Historic disputes over political boundaries will endure. And economic disparities among and within nations will increase as technology and education spread unevenly around the world. The underlying causes of Third World conflict that existed long before the Cold War began remain now that it has ended. They will be compounded by potential strife among states of the former Soviet Union and by continuing tensions in the Middle East. It is just such tensions that in the past fifty years have contributed to 125 wars causing 40 million deaths.

So, in these respects, the world of the future will not be different from the world of the past – conflicts within nations and conflicts among nations will not disappear. But relations between nations will change dramatically. In the post-war years, the United States had the power – and to a considerable degree we exercised that power – to shape the world as we chose. In the next century, that will not be possible.

Japan is destined to play a larger role on the world scene, exercising greater economic and political power and, one hopes, assuming greater economic and political responsibility. The same can be said of Western Europe, following its major step towards economic integration.

And by the middle of the next century, several of the countries, of what in the past we have termed the Third World, will have grown so dramatically in population and economic power as to become major forces in international relations. India is likely to have a population of 1.6 billion; Nigeria 400 million; Brazil 300 million. And if China achieves its ambitious economic goals for the year 2000 (they are likely to be exceeded), and then maintains satisfactory but not spectacular growth rates for the next fifty years, its 1.6 billion people will have the income of

Western Europeans in the 1960s. It will indeed be a power to be reckoned with: economically, politically and militarily.

These figures are of course highly speculative. I point to them simply to emphasize the magnitude and pace of the changes that lie ahead and the need now to adjust our goals, our policies and our institutions to take account of them. In particular, they should make clear that neither the USA nor Japan has even begun to adjust its foreign policy to relate properly to the China it will face in our children's lifetime.

While remaining the world's strongest nation, in the next century the United States will live in a multipolar world, and its foreign policy and defence programmes must be adjusted to this emerging reality. In such a world, need clearly exists for developing new relationships both among the Great Powers and between the Great Powers and other nations.

Many political theorists, in particular those classified as 'realists,' predict a return to traditional power-politics. They argue that the disappearance of ideological competition between East and West will trigger a reversion to traditional relationships based on territorial and economic imperatives. They say that the United States, Russia, Western Europe, China, Japan, and perhaps India will seek to assert themselves in their own regions while still competing for dominance in other areas of the world where conditions are fluid. This view has been expressed, for example, by Harvard Professor Michael Sandel who has written:

> The end of the Cold War does not mean an end of global competition between the Superpowers. Once the ideological dimension fades, what you are left with is not peace and harmony, but old-fashioned global politics based on dominate powers competing for influence and pursuing their internal interests.[2]

Henry Kissinger, also a member of the 'realist' school, has expressed a similar conclusion:

> Victory in the Cold War has propelled America into a world which bears many similarities to the European state system of the eighteenth and nineteenth centuries. ... The absence of both an overriding ideological or strategic threat frees nations to pursue foreign policies based increasingly on their immediate national interest. In an international system characterized by perhaps five or six major powers and a multiplicity of smaller states, order will have to emerge much as it did in past centuries from a reconciliation and balancing of competing national interests.[3]

In contrast to Sandel and Kissinger, Carl Kaysen, former director of the Institute of Advanced Studies at Princeton, has written that:

The international system that relies on the national use of military force as the ultimate guarantor of security, and the threat of its use as the basis of order, is not the only possible one. To seek a different system ... is no longer the pursuit of an illusion, but a necessary effort toward a necessary goal.[4]

Kissinger's and Sandel's conceptions of relations among nations in the post-Cold War world are, of course, historically well founded, but I would argue that they are inconsistent with our increasingly interdependent world. No nation, not even the United States, can stand alone in a world in which nations are inextricably entwined with one another economically, environmentally, and with regard to security. I believe, therefore, that for the future, the United Nations charter offers a far more appropriate framework for international relations than does the doctrine of power politics.

I would argue also that Kissinger and Sandel's emphasis on balance-of-power politics in the twenty-first century assumes we will be willing to continue to accept a foreign policy that lacks a strong moral foundation. I am aware that the majority of political scientists, particularly those who are members of the political realist school, believe morality – as contrasted to a careful calculation of national interests, based on balance-of-power considerations – is a dangerous guide for the establishment of foreign policy. They would say that a foreign policy driven by moral considerations promotes zealousness and a crusading spirit, with potentially dangerous results.

But surely, in the most basic sense, one can apply a moral judgment to the level of killing which occurred in the twentieth century. There can be no justification for it. Nor can there be any justification for its continuation into the twenty-first century. On moral grounds alone, we should act today to prevent such an outcome. A first step would be to establish such an objective as the primary foreign policy goal both for the USA and for the entire human race.

The United States has defined itself in highly idealistic and moral terms throughout its history. We have seen ourselves as defenders of human freedoms across the globe. That feeling was the foundation of Woodrow Wilson's support for normative rules of international behaviour to be administered by a League of Nations. Our moral vision has had an impact on the world. It has led to the formation of a score of international institutions in the economic, social and political fields. But it remains under attack – both within and outside the USA – by those who put greater weight on considerations of narrow national interest.

And many of the most controversial foreign policy debates have found both sides basing their arguments on moral considerations. US policy towards Cuba today is justified on moral grounds by its supporters who say it is immoral to support dictators who abuse human rights. And it is attacked, on moral grounds, by its critics who say it leads to suffering by the mass of the Cuban people. Similarly, a US policy towards China which placed primary emphasis on support of individual civil rights, might well weaken the Chinese government's ability to increase the access of the mass of its population to advances in nutrition, education and health.

Nor do moral considerations offer a clear guide to action in many other foreign policy disputes: *e.g.* the conflicts today in the Middle East or in Bosnia. And even where the moral objective may be clear – as in Rwanda and Burundi where all agree the killing should stop – we may lack the capability to achieve it. We are learning that external military force has limited power to restore a failed state.

Moreover, peoples of different religions and different cultures, confronting common problems, often arrive at different moral judgments relating to conflicts between individual and group rights, between group rights and national rights, and between the rights of individual nations.

So, while there is general acceptance in the USA of the proposition that our foreign policy should advance the welfare of peoples across the globe in terms of political freedom, freedom from want, and preservation of the environment, those objectives are so general that they provide little guidance to addressing the problems that a government confronts each day.

But can we not agree that there is one area of foreign policy in which moral principles should prevail and in which they have not. And that is in relation to the settlement of disputes within nations and among nations without resort to violence.

If so, three specific steps are required:

1. We should reduce the risk of conflict within and among nations by establishing a system of collective security[5] which would have two objectives: the prevention of war and the termination of conflict in the event deterrence fails.
2. The system of collective security should place particular emphasis on limiting the risk of war between or among Great Powers.
3. To avoid the risk of destruction of nations, in the event collective security breaks down, we should redouble our efforts to eliminate weapons of mass destruction, particularly nuclear weapons.

The collective security regime should:

1. Provide all states collective guarantees against external aggression – frontiers would not be changed by force.

2. Codify the rights of minorities and ethnic groups within states – the rights of Moslems in Bosnia, for example – and provide a process by which such groups, who believe their rights have been violated, may seek redress without resort to violence.
3. Establish a mechanism for resolution of both regional conflicts, and conflicts within nations, without unilateral action by the Great Powers. Military force, other than in defence of national territory, would be used only in multilateral actions in accordance with agreed upon norms.

In sum, I believe we should strive to move towards a world in which relations among nations would be based on the rule of law, a world in which conflict-resolution and peace-keeping functions necessary to accomplish these objectives would be performed by multilateral organizations – a reorganized and strengthened United Nations and new and expanded regional organizations.

That is my vision of a system of collective security for the twenty-first century.

Such a vision is easier to articulate than to achieve. The goal is clear; but how to get there is not. And I have no magic formula, no simple road map to success. I do know that such a vision will not be achieved in a month, a year or even a decade. It will be achieved, if at all, slowly and through small steps taken by leaders of dedication and persistence. So I urge that we begin that process now.

Such a world will need leaders.

The leadership role may shift among nations depending on the issue at hand. But more often than not no nation other than the USA will be capable of filling that role. However, we can not succeed in such an endeavour without the co-operation of other nations. And we will not receive that co-operation if we continue to act as though we were omniscient.

We are not.

And yet over and over again – as with respect to Vietnam, Cuba, Iran and Iraq – we act as though we think we are. Failing to obtain the endorsement of other nations, we have applied our power unilaterally. My belief is that the USA should never apply its economic political or military power other than in a multilateral context. The single exception would be in the highly unlikely case of a direct threat to the security of the Continental USA, Alaska or Hawaii.

Whenever the USA accepts leadership in such a multilateral context, it must accept collective decision-making – a concept its people are neither accustomed to nor comfortable with. And other nations – certainly including Japan – must accept a sharing of the risks and costs: the political risks, the financial costs, and the risks of casualties. If the casualities in the Gulf War had been as great as the US Joint Chiefs of Staff originally forecast, 90% of the 'blood cost' would have been borne by the USA while by far the greater part of the benefits – in the form of assured petroleum supply – would have accrued to other nations.

Had the United States and other major powers made clear their commitment to such a system of collective security, and had they stated they would protect nations against attack, the 1990 Iraqi invasion of Kuwait might well have been deterred. Similarly, had the United Nations or NATO taken action, when conflict in the former Yugoslavia erupted in the early 1990s, the ensuing slaughter of tens of thousands of innocent victims might have been prevented.

In the post-Cold War world, operating under a system of collective security, nations – and, in particular, the Great Powers – should be clear about where, and how, they would apply military force. They clearly cannot and should not intervene in every conflict leading to the slaughter of innocent civilians. More than a dozen wars currently rage throughout the world. And other serious conflicts may soon break out elsewhere. Where, if at all, should the Great Powers and/or the United Nations be involved? Neither the United States nor any other Great Power has a clear answer to that question. The answers can be developed only through intense debate, over a period of years, within the USA, among the other Great Powers, and in the councils of international organizations.

The rules governing response to aggression across national borders can be relatively simple and clear. But those relating to attempts to maintain or restore political order and to prevent wholesale slaughter within nations – as, for instance, within Rwanda or Burundi – are far less so.

Criteria determining the use of US military forces should be derived from a precise statement of US foreign policy objectives. For forty years our objective remained clear: to contain an expansionist Soviet Union. But that can no longer be the focus of our efforts. We have lost our enemy. What will we put in its place? President Clinton told the UN General Assembly on September 27, 1993: 'Our overriding purpose must be to expand and strengthen the world's community of market-based democracies.' Anthony Lake, the national security adviser, echoed this a short time later when he stated that 'the successor to a doctrine of containment must be a strategy of enlargement – enlargement of the world's free community of market democracies.' Such a general formulation of our objectives is not sufficient.

The United States cannot and should not intervene in every conflict arising from a nation's attempt to move towards capitalist democracy. For example, we were surely correct not to support with military force Eduard Shevardnadze's attempt to install democracy in Georgia. Nor can we be expected to try to stop by military force every instance of the slaughter of innocent civilians.

Several crucial questions must be faced. To what degree of human suffering should we respond? Under a UN convention, formalized in a global treaty in 1989, the United States agreed to join in stopping genocide. But what constitutes genocide? In June 1994, the US government, while recognizing the killing of over 200,000 Rwandans as 'acts of genocide,' refused to state that the killing fell under the treaty's provisions.[6] And would there not be other cases, short of genocide, that would also justify intervention? At what point should we intervene – as preventive diplomacy fails and killing appears likely, or only when the slaughter is increasing? How should we respond when nations involved in such conflicts – as was the case in the former Yugoslavia – claim that outside intervention clearly infringes on their sovereignty? We have seen regional organizations – in particular, the Organization of African Unity and the Organization of American States – time and time again fail to support such intervention.

Above all else, the criteria governing intervention should recognize a lesson we should have learned in Vietnam: external military force has only a limited capacity to facilitate the process of nation building.

It should be made clear to our people that such questions will, at best, require years to answer. But we should force the debate within our own nation and within international forums. Some of the issues may never be resolved. There may be times when we must recognize that we cannot right all wrongs.

If we are to achieve the objective of avoiding in the twenty-first century the tragic loss of life we have just lived through, above all else, special emphasis must be placed on avoiding conflict among the Great Powers.

Excluding the end of the Cold War, I believe the two most important geo-political events of the past fifty years have been the reconciliation between France and Germany, after centuries of enmity, and the establishment of peaceful relations between Japan and the US, after one of the bloodiest conflicts in the modern era. It is inconceivable today that either Germany or Japan would engage in war with any of the Great Powers of the Western world. Can we not move to integrate both Russia and China into the family of nations in ways that make war between them and the other Great Powers equally unlikely.

We have not done so.

The expansion of NATO is viewed by many Russian leaders as a threat to their security. At a time when the nation's military forces – both conventional and nuclear – have been severally weakened, they see NATO planning to move its forces eastwards. This has strengthened the position of their hard-line nationalists, increased their feelings of xenophobia, and, through the scrapping of their doctrine of 'No First Use,' led to a more aggressive nuclear policy. George Kennan has stated that NATO expansion will prove to be one of the greatest foreign policy mistakes made by the West since the end of the Second World War. I agree with him.

Similarly, China has viewed the action taken in 1997 by Japan and the USA to extend – and, in the words of the Chinese, 'to expand' – the US-Japan Security Treaty as a hostile act. In 1997, Prime Minister Li Peng stated very emphatically to my associates and I, during a visit to his country, that whereas, initially, the Treaty might have been directed against the Soviet Union, with the end of the Cold War it could have no purpose other than to contain and, ultimately, threaten China. He supported his argument by emphasizing that, contrary to the action of Germany, Japan had never admitted or accepted responsibility for its role in the Second World War. He claimed – perhaps with exaggeration – that Japan was responsible for 20 million Chinese dead. And he said he observed continuing signs of militarism in Japanese society.

Dangerous frustrations also exist between China and the USA arising from divergent policies towards Taiwan, North Korea and the East Asia Region.

My associates and I were shocked by the vehemence with which the Chinese stated their views. I mention them here to illustrate how far both we and the Japanese have to go before we can establish a pattern of relations with China comparable to those that exist between France and Germany and between the USA and Japan.

I turn now to the third of the three actions to which I urge immediate attention be directed: action to avoid the risk of destruction of nations, through the use of weapons of mass destruction, in particular, nuclear weapons, in the event that collective security breaks down.

Today, nine years after the end of the Cold War, there are approximately 40,000 nuclear warheads in the world with a destructive power more than one million times greater than the bomb that flattened Hiroshima. We in the USA – and all other inhabitants of our globe – continue to live with the risk of nuclear destruction. The United States' war plans provide for contingent use of nuclear weapons just as they did when I was Secretary of Defense in the 1960s. But I do not believe that the average American recognizes this fact. No doubt, he or she was surprised and pleased by the announcement of the START I nuclear arms control treaty, which was signed by the USA and Russia in 1991. When finally implemented it will reduce the arsenal to approximately 20,000 weapons. In June 1992, Bush and Yeltsin agreed to START II which would further reduce the total to 10,000. In March 1997, they spoke of going still lower to a level of 6000. But START II has not been and may never be ratified.

Moreover, even if it, and the further reductions discussed in 1997, were to be approved by the Congress and the Duma, the risk of destruction of societies across the globe, while somewhat reduced, would be far from eliminated. I doubt that a survivor – if there was one – could perceive much difference between a world in which 6000 nuclear warheads had been exploded and one subject to attack by 40,000. So the question is can we not go further? Surely the answer must be yes.

The end of the Cold War, along with the growing understanding of the lack of utility of nuclear weapons and of the high risk associated with their continued existence, points to both the opportunity and the urgency with which the nuclear powers should re-examine their long-term nuclear force objectives. We should begin with a broad public debate over alternative nuclear strategies. I believe such a debate should open with a discussion of the moral issues relating to the use of nuclear weapons by the five declared nuclear powers.

As I stated earlier, most political scientists and most security experts oppose introducing moral considerations into discussions of international relations and defence policy. And I will admit that in many situations they provide ambiguous guidance at best. But surely the human race should be prepared to accept that it is totally immoral for one nation, no matter what the provocation, to believe it – through its leader, acting alone – has the right to initiate action that will destroy another nation. And would it not be even more morally unacceptable if such action by one belligerent would destroy not only the other belligerent, but – through the spread of radioactive fallout – non-belligerent nations across the globe as well. Yet that would have been the result if either Russia or the USA had implemented the nuclear strategy that each nation followed for forty years and continues to follow today.

The debate should then move beyond moral considerations to a detailed examination of the military utility of nuclear weapons and of the off-setting military risks of their use. I believe it would support the conclusion that we should move back to a non-nuclear world.

In support of my position, I will make three points:

1. The experience of the Cuban Missile Crisis in 1962 – and, in particular, what has been learned about it recently – makes clear that

so long as we and other Great Powers possess large inventories of nuclear weapons, we will face the risk of their use and the destruction of our nation.

2. That risk is no longer – if it ever was – justifiable on military grounds.

3. In recent years, there has been a dramatic change in the thinking of leading Western security experts – both military and civilian – regarding the military utility of nuclear weapons. More and more of them – although certainly not yet a majority – are expressing views similar to those I have stated.

First, the Cuban Missile Crisis.

It is now widely recognized that the actions of the Soviet Union, Cuba, and the United States in October 1962 brought the three nations to the verge of war. But what was not known then, and is not widely understood today, was how close the world came to the brink of nuclear disaster. In 1997, the Kennedy Library released heretofore highly classified tapes[7] which provided new insights into the near catastrophe from a US point of view. A few months before that, a similar account of Khrushchev's state of mind was published.[8] Both accounts are frightening. Neither the Soviet Union nor the United States intended, by its actions, to create the risks they both incurred.

You may recall that the crisis began when the Soviets moved nuclear missiles and bombers to Cuba – secretly and with the clear intent to deceive – in the summer and early fall of 1962. The missiles were to be targeted against cities along America's east coast, putting 90 million Americans at risk. Photographs taken by a U-2 reconnaissance aircraft on Sunday, October 14, 1962 brought the deployments to President Kennedy's attention. He and his military and civilian security advisers believed that the Soviets' action posed a threat to the West. Kennedy therefore authorized a naval quarantine of Cuba to be effective Wednesday, October 24. Preparations also began for air strikes and an amphibious invasion. The contingency plans called for a 'first-day' air attack of 1080 sorties, a huge attack. An invasion force totalling 180,000 troops was assembled in southeastern US ports. The crisis came to a head on Saturday, October 27 and Sunday, October 28. Had Khrushchev not publicly announced on that Sunday that he was removing the missiles, I believe that on Monday a majority of Kennedy's military and civilian advisers would have recommended launching the attacks.

To understand what caused the crisis – and how to avoid similar ones in the future – high-ranking Soviet, Cuban and American participants in the decisions relating to it met in a series of conferences beginning in

1987. The meetings extended over a period of five years. One chaired by Fidel Castro in Havana in January 1992 was the fifth and last.

By the conclusion of the third meeting in Moscow, it had become clear that the decisions of each of the three nations, before and during the crisis, had been distorted by misinformation, miscalculation, and misjudgment. I shall cite only four of many examples:

1. Before Soviet missiles were introduced into Cuba in the summer of 1962, the Soviet Union and Cuba believed the United States intended to invade the island in order to overthrow Castro and remove his government. But we had no such intention.
2. The United States believed the Soviets would never move nuclear warheads outside the Soviet Union – they never had – but in fact they did. In Moscow, in 1989, we learned that by October 1962, although the CIA at the time was reporting no nuclear weapons on the island, Soviet nuclear warheads had, indeed, been delivered to Cuba. As I have said, they were to be targeted on US cities.
3. The Soviets believed that nuclear weapons could be introduced into Cuba secretly, without detection, and that the USA would not respond when their presence was disclosed. There, too, they were in error.
4. Finally, those who were prepared to urge President Kennedy to destroy the missiles by a US air attack which, in all likelihood, would have been followed by an amphibious invasion, were almost certainly mistaken in their belief that the Soviets would not respond militarily. At the time, the CIA reported 10,000 Soviet troops in Cuba. At the Moscow conference, we learned there were in fact 43,000 Soviet troops on the island, along with 270,000 well-armed Cuban troops. Both forces, in the words of their commanders, were determined to 'fight to the death.' The Cuban officials estimated they would have suffered 100,000 causalities. The Soviets – including long-term Foreign Minister Andrei A. Gromyko and former Ambassador to the USA Anatoly Dobrynin – expressed utter disbelief that we would have thought that, in the face of such a catastrophic defeat, they would not have responded militarily somewhere in the world. Very probably, the result would have been uncontrollable escalation.

By the end of that meeting in Moscow, we had agreed we could draw two lessons from our discussions:

1. In the face of nuclear weapons, crisis management is inherently dangerous, difficult, and uncertain; and
2. Due to misjudgment, misinformation and miscalculation of the kind I

have referred to, it is not possible to predict with confidence the consequences of military action between Great Powers armed with such weapons. Therefore, we must direct our attention and energies to crisis avoidance.

In 1962, during the crisis, some of us – particularly President Kennedy and I – believed the United States faced great danger. The Moscow meeting confirmed that judgement. But during the Havana conference, we learned that both of us – and certainly others – had seriously underestimated those dangers. While in Havana, we were told by the former Warsaw Pact Chief of Staff, General Anatoly Gribkov, that, in 1962, Soviet forces in Cuba possessed not only nuclear warheads for the intermediate-range missiles targeted on US cities, but nuclear bombs and tactical nuclear warheads as well. The tactical warheads were to be used against US invasion forces. At the time, as I mentioned, the CIA was reporting no warheads on the island.

In November 1992 – 30 years after the event – we learned more. An article appeared in the Russian press which stated that, at the height of the Missile Crisis, Soviet forces on Cuba possessed a total of 162 nuclear warheads, including at least 90 tactical warheads. Moreover, it was reported that, on October 26, 1962 – a moment of great tension – warheads were moved from their storage sites to positions closer to their delivery vehicles in anticipation of a US invasion.[9] The next day, Soviet Defence Minister Malinovsky received a cable from General Pliyev, the Soviet commander in Cuba, informing him of this action. Malinovsky sent it to Khrushchev. Khrushchev returned it to Malinovsky with 'Approved' scrawled across the document. Clearly, there was a high risk that, in the face of a US attack – which, as I have said, many in the US government, military and civilian alike, were prepared to recommend to President Kennedy – the Soviet forces in Cuba would have decided to use their nuclear weapons rather than lose them.[10]

We need not speculate about what would have happened in that event. We can predict the results with certainty.

Although a US invasion force would not have been equipped with tactical nuclear warheads – the President and I had specifically prohibited that – no one should believe that had American troops been attacked with nuclear weapons, the USA would have refrained from a nuclear response. And where would it have ended? In utter disaster.

The point I wish to emphasize is this: human beings are fallible. We know we all make mistakes. In our daily lives, mistakes are costly, but we try to learn from them. In conventional war, they cost lives, sometimes thousands of lives. But if mistakes were to affect decisions relating to the use of nuclear forces, there would be no learning period. They would result in the destruction of nations. I believe, therefore, it can be predicted with confidence that the indefinite combination of human fallibility and nuclear weapons carries a very high risk of a potential nuclear catastrophe.[11]

Is there a military justification for continuing to accept that risk? The answer is 'No.'

Proponents of nuclear weapons have produced only one plausible scenario for initiating their use: a situation where there is no prospect of retaliation. That means either against a non-nuclear state or against one so weakly armed as to permit the user to have full confidence in his nuclear forces' capability to achieve a totally disarming first strike. But even such circumstances have not, in fact, provided a sufficient basis for the use of nuclear weapons in war. For example, although American forces were in desperate straits twice during the Korean War – first immediately following the North Korean attack in 1950 and then when the Chinese crossed the Yalu – the United States did not use nuclear weapons. At that time, North Korea and China had no nuclear capability and the Soviet Union only a negligible one.

The conclusion is clear: the military utility of nuclear weapons is limited to deterring one's opponent from their use.[12] Therefore, if our opponent has no nuclear weapons, there is no need for us to possess them.

Partly because of the increased understanding of how close we came to disaster during the Missile Crisis, but also because of a growing recognition of the lack of military utility of the weapons, there has been a revolutionary change in thinking about the role of nuclear forces. Much of this change has occurred in the past five years. Many military leaders are now prepared to go far beyond the Bush-Yeltsin agreement. Some go so far as to state, as I have, that the long-term objective should be a return to a non-nuclear world.[13]

That is, however, a very controversial proposition. A majority of Western security experts – both military and civilian – continue to believe that the threat of the use of nuclear weapons prevents war. Zbigniew Brzezinski, President Carter's National Security Adviser, has argued that a plan for eliminating nuclear weapons 'is a plan for making the world safe for conventional warfare. I am therefore not enthusiastic about it.' A report of an advisory committee, appointed by former Defense Secretary Richard Cheney and chaired by former Air Force Secretary Thomas Reed, made essentially the same point.[14] Clearly the current Administration supports that position.[15] However, even if one accepts that argument, it must be recognized that the deterrent to conventional force aggression carries a very high long-term cost: the risk of a nuclear exchange.

It is that risk – which to me is unacceptable – that is leading prominent security experts to change their views. I doubt that the public is aware of these changes. They have been reflected in numerous unclassified, but not widely disseminated, statements. I will cite only a few.

Four recent reports, three of which I have referred to above, all recommend major changes in nuclear strategies and drastic reductions in nuclear force levels.

1. The Spring 1993 issue of Foreign Affairs carried an article, co-authored by retired Chairman of the Joint Chiefs of Staff, Admiral William J. Crowe, Jr., which concluded that by the year 2000, the USA and Russia could reduce strategic nuclear forces to 1000-1500 warheads each. The article was later expanded into a book which added; 'Nor is 1000-1500 the lowest level obtainable by the early 21st Century.' [16]

2. In December 1995, the Stimson Center Report, signed by four recently retired four-star officers, recommended moving through a series of four steps to the 'goal of elimination' of nuclear weapons.[17]

3. The Canberra Commission, which was appointed by Prime Minister Keating of Australia, recommended in 1996 'a programme to achieve a world totally free of nuclear weapons.' The Commission members included, among others: Michel Rocard, the former prime minister of France; Joseph Rotblat, the 1995 Nobel Peace Laureate and one of the designers of the original nuclear bomb; Field Marshal Lord Carver, former Chief of the British Defence Staff; General Lee Butler, former commander of the US Strategic Air Command; and myself. The Commission's recommendations were unanimous. They were presented without any qualification or even the slightest note of dissent.

4. The National Academy of Sciences Report (1997) stated that reductions by the USA and Russia, within a few years, to a level of 2000 warheads each 'should be easily accommodated within the existing and anticipated strategic force structures of both sides.' It then recommended moving to 1000 warheads each and later to 'roughly 300 each.'

These four reports should not have come as surprises. For nearly twenty years, more and more Western military and civilian security experts have expressed doubts about the military utility of nuclear weapons. This is what they have said:

1. By 1982, five of the seven retired Chiefs of the British Defence Staff expressed their belief that initiating the use of nuclear weapons, in accordance with NATO policy, would lead to disaster. Lord Louis Mountbatten, Chief of Staff from 1959-1965, said a few months before he was murdered in 1979: 'As a military man I can see no use for any nuclear weapons.' And Field Marshal Lord Carver, Chief of Staff from 1973-1976, wrote in 1982 that he was totally opposed to NATO ever initiating the use of nuclear weapons.[18]

2. Henry Kissinger, speaking in Brussels in 1979, made quite clear he believed the United States would never initiate a nuclear strike against the Soviet Union, no matter what the provocation. 'Our European allies,' he said, 'should not keep asking us to multiply strategic assurances that we cannot possibly mean or if we do mean we should not execute because if we execute we risk the destruction of civilization.'[19]

3. Melvin Laird, President Nixon's first Secretary of Defense, was reported in The Washington Post of April 12, 1982 as saying: 'A worldwide zero nuclear option with adequate verification should now be our goal ... These weapons ... are useless for military purposes.'

4. Former West German Chancellor Helmut Schmidt stated in a 1987 BBC interview: 'Flexible response [NATO's strategy calling for the use of nuclear weapons in response to a Warsaw Pact attack by non-nuclear forces] is nonsense. Not out of date, but nonsense ... The Western idea, which was created in the 1950s, that we should be willing to use nuclear weapons first, in order to make up for our so-called conventional deficiency, has never convinced me.'[20]

5. Admiral Noel Gaylor, former Commander-in-Chief of US air, ground, and sea forces in the Pacific, remarked in 1987: 'There is no sensible military use of any of our nuclear forces. The only reasonable use is to deter our opponents from using his nuclear forces.'

6. General Larry Welch, former US Air Force Chief of Staff and previously Commander of the Strategic Air Command, recently put the same thought in these words: 'Nuclear deterrence depended on someone believing that you would commit an act totally irrational if done.'[21]

7. In July 1994, General Charles A. Horner, then chief of the US Space Command, stated: 'The nuclear weapon is obsolete. I want to get rid of them all.'[22]

8. December 5, 1996, nineteen senior retired US military officers and 42 senior admirals and generals from other nations across the world stated their support for complete elimination of nuclear weapons.

9. February 2, 1998, one hundred and nineteen present and former heads

of state and other senior civilian leaders – including, for example, Helmut Schmidt, Michel Rocard, James Callaghan, Jimmy Carter and six former Prime Ministers of Japan – endorsed a similar statement.

In the early 1960s, I had reached conclusions similar to those which I have cited. In long private conversations, first with President Kennedy and then with President Johnson, I had recommended, without qualification, that they never initiate, under any circumstances, the use of nuclear weapons.[23] I believe they accepted my recommendations. But neither they nor I could discuss our positions publicly because they were totally contrary to established NATO policy.

In truth, for over thirty years, with respect to our stated nuclear policy, it could have been said 'The Emperor Had No Clothes.' I do not believe that after 1960, by which time the Soviets had acquired a survivable retaliatory force, any one of our Presidents – Eisenhower, Kennedy, Johnson, Nixon, Ford, Carter, Reagan, Bush or Clinton – would ever have initiated the use of nuclear weapons. Nor would our allies have wished them to do so. To initiate a nuclear strike against a comparable equipped opponent would have been tantamount to committing suicide. To initiate use against a non-nuclear opponent would have been militarily unnecessary, politically indefensible and morally repugnant.

It was the acceptance of that judgment that led the Canberra Commission to recommend the complete elimination of nuclear weapons.

But the Commission went further. It accepted the evidence that the current nuclear posture of both Russia and the USA poses a totally unacceptable danger to the two countries and indeed to the peace of the world. A report by Bruce G. Blair of The Brookings Institution graphically describes the danger.[24] Blair states that both the USA and Russia keep thousands of nuclear warheads on 'hair trigger' alert, poised for launch before the opposing side's missiles reach their targets. The 'launch on warning' doctrine requires that in less than 15 minutes a missile attack be detected and analysed, the decision to retaliate made, and orders to do so disseminated to hundreds of weapons sites. The risk of accidental, inadvertent or unauthorized launch would exist under the best of conditions. But today, according to Russia's own commanders, their country's alert position is particularly vulnerable. Their command posts will not survive attack, much of their early-warning network is not functioning; safeguards against unauthorized use of nuclear forces are ineffective, large numbers of both their land-based and sea-based forces are inoperative; and the majority of the remainder would not survive a US counterforce attack. The situation in Blair's words, is 'extremely dangerous.' Both the USA and Russia, while seeking to deter a vanishing risk of deliberate nuclear aggression, are running a growing risk of stumbling into an inadvertent nuclear war.

The Canberra Commission came to the same conclusion.

Therefore, with the strong support of its two military chiefs (Field Marshal Lord Carver and former US Strategic Air Command Commander General Lee Butler), it urged that the five declared nuclear powers – China, Russia, Britain, France and the United States – not only state their unequivocal political commitment to the elimination of nuclear weapons, but accompany that commitment with three immediate steps consistent with fulfilling it:

1. The removal of all nuclear weapons from alert status.
2. The separation of all nuclear warheads from their launch vehicles.
3. A declaration of 'No First Use' of nuclear weapons against nuclear states, and 'No Use' against non-nuclear nations.

Years will pass before the Commission's recommendations are fully implemented. But we are beginning to break out of the mindset that has guided the strategy of the nuclear powers for over four decades. More and more political and military leaders are coming to understand two fundamental truths:

1. We can indeed 'put the genie back in the bottle.'
2. If we do not, there is a substantial and unacceptable risk that the twenty-first century will witness a nuclear holocaust.

In sum, with the end of the Cold War, if we act to establish a system of collective security, and if we take steps to return to a non-nuclear world, the twenty-first century, while certainly not a century of tranquillity, need not witness the killing, by war, of another 160 (or even 300) million people. Surely that must be not only our hope, not only our dream, but our steadfast objective. I know that some – perhaps many – may consider such a statement so naive, so simplistic, and so idealistic as to be quixotic. But as human beings, citizens with power to influence events in the world, can we be at peace with ourselves if we strive for less? I think not.

I wish to dedicate this essay to Joseph Rotblat on his 90th birthday. If the human race avoids nuclear catastrophe in the twenty-first century, few individuals will deserve more credit than he. He has fought – often almost alone – for elimination of nuclear weapons for more than fifty years.

Notes and References

1. 'Preventing Deadly Conflict, Final Report' Carnegie Commission on Preventing Deadly Conflict, Carnegie Corporation, New York, December 1997, p. xii.
2. *New York Times*, 31 December 1989.
3. Henry Kissinger, *Diplomacy*, New York: Simon and Schuster, 1994, p. 805.
4. Carl Kaysen, 'Is War Obsolete?' *International Security* 14(4): 63, Spring 1990.
5. I have included in my concept of 'collective security' elements of what Janne Nolan refers to as 'co-operative security' (see Chapter One 'Global Engagement' by John Steinbruner, Ash Carter, Bill Perry, Janne Nolan, *et al*, Brookings, 1996). Ms. Nolan states, 'one strategy does not preclude the other and both are, in fact, initially reinforcing.'
6. *Washington Post*, June 11, 1994, p. A1.
7. 'The Kennedy Tapes,' Ernest R. May and Philip D. Zelikow, Belknap, Harvard University, 1997.
8. 'One Hell of a Gamble,' Aleksandr Fursenko and Timothy Naftali, New York: Norton, 1997.
9. General Gribkov elaborated on these points at a meeting in the Wilson Center, Washington D.C. on April 5, 1994.
10. See Anatoly Dokochaev, 'Afterword to Sensational 100 Day Nuclear Cruise,' Krasnaya Zvezda, November 6, 1992, p. 2 and V. Badurikin interview with Dimitri Volkogonov in 'Operation Anadyr,' Trud, October 27, 1992, p. 3.
11. Both the Canberra Commission and the Carnegie Commission came to the same conclusion. Using almost identical words they state: 'The position that large numbers of nuclear weapons can be retained in perpetuity and never used – accidentally or by decision – defies credibility.' (Report of the Canberra Commission on the Elimination of Nuclear Weapons, Commonwealth of Australia, 1996, p.18; 'Preventing Deadly Conflict ...,' *op. cit.*, p. 70.)
12. This statement was endorsed by the US National Academy of Sciences in 1991 in a report signed by 18 security experts including David C. Jones former Chief of Staff of the US Air Force ('The Future of the US-Soviet Nuclear Relationship,' Washington, D.C.: National Academy Press, p. 3); by the Stimson Center's Panel on Nuclear Forces chaired by the former SACEUR, General Andrew Goodpaster ('An Evolving Nuclear Posture,' Stimson Center, Washington D.C., December 1995, p. 15); and by the Canberra Commission (Report of the Canberra Commission, *op. cit.* p. 18).
13. I recognize, of course, that the abolition of nuclear weapons would not be possible without development of an adequate verification system. Are acceptable verification regimes feasible? The decision point on whether verification is adequate for complete elimination (as opposed, for example to reductions to a level of say 100 warheads), is not likely to be resolved for some time. In the end, comparative risks must be evaluated. The Canberra Commission, which also recommended abolition, concluded that the risk of

use of the weapons far exceeds the risks associated with whatever nuclear force a cheating state could assemble before it was exposed.

14. See John J. Fialks and Frederick Kemps, 'US Welcomes Soviet Arms Plan, but Dismisses Pact as Propaganda,' *Wall Street Journal*, January 17, 1986; Thomas C. Reed and Michael O. Wheeler, 'The Role of Nuclear Weapons in the New World Order,' December 1991.

15. See William Perry's statement to the Stimson Center, September 20, 1994; and Department of Defense briefing, September 22, 1994.

16. McGeorge Bundy, William J. Crowe, Jr., and Sidney O. Drell, *Reducing Nuclear Danger: The Road Away from the Brink*, New York: Council on Foreign Relations Press, 1993, p. 100.

17. 'An Evolving Nuclear Posture,' *op. cit.*

18. See Solly Zuckerman, *Nuclear Illusions and Reality,* New York: Viking, 1982, p. 70; and *The Sunday Times*, February 21, 1982.

19. Henry Kissinger, 'NATO Defence and the Soviet Threat,' *Survival*, November-December 1979, p. 266.

20. BBC Radio interview with Stuart Simon, July 16, 1987.

21. Larry Welch to Adam Scheinman, March 21, 1994.

22. *Boston Globe*, July 16, 1994.

23. Robert S. McNamara, 'The Military Role of Nuclear Weapons,' *Foreign Affairs*, Fall 1983, p. 79.

24. 'De-alerting Strategic Nuclear Forces' a preliminary draft of a study of nuclear forces presented by Bruce Blair on January 29, 1998 to The Independent Task Force on Reducing the Risk of Nuclear War.

10

From a Nuclear-Free to a War-Free World

Anatol Rapoport

Throughout the decades of the Cold War, awareness of the threat presented by nuclear weapons grew both in breadth and acuteness, boosted as it was by recurrent crises, to the point where a nuclear holocaust appeared imminent. When the Cold War ended, the threat seemed to recede, not surprisingly, since confrontations between the nuclear powers (as in Berlin 1948-49 or in the Caribbean in 1962) seemed no longer likely. However, campaigns pressing for elimination of nuclear weapons intensified. The emphasis shifted from the immediate danger posed by the weapons to the refutation of justifications for keeping them whether as weapons in war or as backers of deterrence. Resistance to this pressure by military establishments and their supporting institutions also intensified. Outlines of a confrontation between world public opinion and institutions comprising the infrastructure of the 'war system' became ever more clearly discernible. In what follows I will offer an interpretation of this confrontation and suggest opportunities created by it for pursuing the goal of a war-free world.

Three Philosophies of Peace

Three philosophies of peace are discernible throughout history, which could be appropriately called pacifism, peacemaking and abolitionism. Each stems from a different perception of the origins of violence, conflict, aggression, in short, of conceptions, behaviour patterns, attitudes, or affects underlying war.

The pacifist sees these origins within the psyche of the human individual; the peacemaker in the interaction between usually pairs of individuals, groups or nations; the abolitionist sees the roots of war in the evolution of its infrastructure, specifically of its war-making institutions.

Among the exponents of pacifism in antiquity were founders of world religions – Jesus of Nazareth in the West, and Siddhartha Gautama (Buddha) in the East. In our era, the most articulate interpreter of the pacifist teaching of Jesus was Leo Tolstoy. Peace, according to these teachers, is attained by purging the soul (mind, psyche) of conflict or hostility. Tolstoy, in particular, emphasized unconditional love of Other as the foundation of peace among humans. Pacifism, that is, categorical rejection of war on moral grounds in all circumstances, is the society-oriented expression of this attitude. It is represented in our day by several religious sects, such as Mennonites and Dukhobors (offsprings of Christianity), the Baha'i, (offspring of Islam), and Soka Gakkai (a secular offspring of Buddhism). A prominent feature common to many pacifist communities is refusal to serve in the armed forces.

Peacemaking, also called conflict resolution, is the orientation underlying attempts to prevent, stop or contain overt violence at individual, group, societal or international level by arbitration or mediation (in specific instances) or a formally established framework of cooperation (in the long run). The fundamental underlying assumption of peacemaking is that conflicts of all degrees of severity, including war are generated by clashing interests. Accordingly, the task of the peacemaker is to find some way of reconciling these interests. Not identification of self with other (the pacifist ideal), but finding a mutually acceptable middle ground between the positions or some area of coinciding interests is thought to be the key to forestalling violence.

Among the peacemakers of the millennium presently drawing to a close, we find Vladimir Monomach, a Kievan prince, who unsuccessfully tried to end the perpetual internecine strife among Russian princes in 1097. Some 370 years later, King George of Bohemia attempted to establish a peace covenant among the Christian princes of Europe. One Hiawatha, a possibly legendary but possibly historical chieftain of the Onondaga tribe in North America, supposedly a contemporary of George of Bohemia, has been credited by tradition for organizing a peace pact among six tribes, forming the Iroquois Federation.

In our day, we find peacemaking mostly in the form of crisis defusion, such as of the Suez crisis (at the initiative of Lester Pearson of Canada); of one of the periodic crises involving India and Pakistan (at the initiative of Alexei Kosygin of the USSR); of the crisis generated by the uprising (*intifada*) of the Palestinians against Israeli occupation (at the initiative of

Johann Holst of Norway – the so called Oslo Accords). An attempt by President Clinton of the USA to sustain the so called 'peace process' based on the Oslo Accords, can also be subsumed under peacemaking.

Of the pacifist religious sects, the Quakers have been the most active in peace-making. They played an important, though intentionally inconspicuous, part in bringing about a rapprochement between the two Germanies and in ending the civil war in Nigeria.[1]

Neither persuading individuals to reject violence, nor ad hoc efforts to prevent or alleviate violence are central to the goals pursued by abolitionists. Rather, the central goal is the dismantling of the *war system*, which appears in the light of that outlook as the prime generator of wars and related forms of massive violence.

Relative Efficacy of the Three Approaches

The proselytizing of personal pacifism is hampered by two limitations. First, the rate of individual 'conversions' to pacifism is extremely slow, probably far slower than the growth of the general population. Moreover, such conversions are very likely limited to those who are already predisposed to pacifism. On the other hand, arguments against pacifism seem convincing to those who are opposed to it on whatever grounds. The most common one is the old saw that 'You can't change human nature.' A sophisticated version of this homily is offered by some sociobiologists, who point out that, in all likelihood, a drive for aggression was selected for in the process of evolution, at least in males of most vertebrates, because of the reproductive advantage it confers in competition for mates or territory; and there is no reason to suppose that humans are an exception. There are, to be sure, counter-arguments to the effect that physical combat for possession of females has long been abandoned, or to the effect that human behaviour is shaped by cultural evolution much more rapidly and effectively than by biological evolution.

The second limitation stems from the observation that arguments of this sort are hardly relevant to the central problem – banning war as a pervasive feature of human existence. The reason for this is that hatred, aggressiveness and related affects are becoming increasingly irrelevant to the conduct of war. This decoupling of war from affects usually assumed to underlie its inception and conduct has been clearly a consequence of evolution, not, however, of the human psyche but of war technology. It takes much less hatred to kill some one with a rifle than with a machete, and even less to kill with artillery or aviation, when you cannot see the victims.

During the Vietnam war, General W. Westmoreland wrote:

On the battlefield of the future, enemy forces will be located and targeted almost instantaneously through the use of data banks, computer assisted intelligence evaluation, and automated fire control. With first round kill probabilities approaching certainty, and with surveillance devices that can continuously track the enemy, the need for large forces to fix the opposition physically will be less important.[2]

It is easy to imagine the realization of this prediction in the context of a nuclear exchange. Unarmed people sit far underground watching signals on screens which they have learned to interpret and react to by moving appropriate levers, buttons or whatever. This is their entire battle experience. They are completely insulated from the effects of their routine actions. It is only a step to replacing these humans with robots, completely impervious to appeals, such as 'Remember your humanity' a motto adopted by the Pugwash movement. Ironically, the prediction of the little girl, who said 'Some day they will give a war and nobody will come' may really be almost realized, but not the anticipated results.

In sum, the effectiveness of pacifism as an antidote to war is limited for two reasons. First, the technology of homicide has progressively separated warmaking from violence-generating passions and thus has immunized humans against attempts to make them peaceful by liberating them from those passions. It is fair to say that in our day you don't have to hate anyone to kill everyone. Second, the technology of omnicide may make the recruitment of millions in the service of killing unnecessary and so may make conscientious objection to bearing arms (a major goal of traditional pacifist proselytizing) irrelevant.

In contrast to the limitations of pacifism as an antidote to war, those of conflict resolution are less apparent. While many students of war dismiss the notion that a cardinal source of war is inherent aggressiveness of humans (or at least of men), by far the most seek the roots of war in clashes of interests. Indeed, 'causes' of war are identified in this view as relations among states during a span of history preceding some war. The events assumed to trigger it are usually the focus of expositions found in history books, encyclopedias, and other sources. The implications of this conception for the 'peacemaking' philosophy of peace are clear. It is assumed that peacemaking can be made more effective by applying results of research on the 'causes of war.' Accordingly, the task of peace research appears to be analogous to that of medical research. Disease is prevented or cured by discovering and removing its underlying causes. So it is assumed that war can be prevented by understanding the genesis of the issues over which it is fought or threatened, and by learning to resolve them. This, in the view of the peacemaker, ought to be a main task of political science and diplomacy.

The 'rationalist' approach can be said to have been the mainstream of peace philosophy since the idea of 'progress' pervaded Western civilization. In the late nineteenth century one S. Amos wrote:

> ... the teachings of history are to the effect that practices and institutions which at the time seem to be necessary conditions of social and political conditions of all people, and yet stand condemned as counter to principles of justice and political expedience, vanish in an almost inconceivable short space of time, and become so obsolete as to be with difficulty revived even in imagination.[3]

Further, the author conjectures that before the obsolete institution disappears altogether, its harmful effects will be attenuated. In particular, war will become progressively more humane.

> ... the modes of conducting Wars between ... civilized states have been steadily undergoing changes in one continuous direction, the object of these changes being the diminution of miseries inherent in warfare, the limitation of its means, and the alleviation of evils incidentally occasioned by it to the Neutral States.[4]

Finally, the author contends that one need only apply control guided by knowledge in order to abolish war altogether.

Even if there are those who regard all hopes for a time of permanent peace utopian, it is not denied in any quarter that there are general causes that produce both peace and war and that these causes can, to some extent be controlled so as to foster the one and not the other.

Looking back on the century drawing to a close, we see on the one hand a solid confirmation of Amos's hypothesis concerning attitudes towards war and on the other a dramatic disconfirmation of his prognoses. The institution of war has indeed lost most of its moral justification. Hardly anyone ventures in our day to glorify or romanticize war. War is now almost universally regarded as a disaster even by those who would unleash it or conduct it under appropriate conditions. On the other hand, Amos's, prognoses about progressive humanization of war and of mobilizing knowledge and rationality in the service of peacemaking could be interpreted as mockery, were they not made in all seriousness by so many of his contemporaries. Indeed, on the very eve of the First World War the Eleventh Edition of the Encyclopedia Britannica had this to say on the subject of Peace:

Peace until quite recently was merely the political condition which prevailed in the intervals between wars. It is now customary among writers on international law to give peace at any rate a volume in itself... The rise of arbitration as a method of settling international difficulties has carried it a step further... [T]he preservation of peace has become an object of direct political effort. The methods of insuring such preservation are now almost as precise as the methods of war.

Looking back on our century, we see that neither the changed attitudes towards war nor the supposed perfection of methods of peacemaking were accompanied either by 'humanization' of war, or by reduction of its frequency or of its lethality. Estimates of the total number of war-related deaths during the century range up to 160 million, of which non-combatants constitute nearly 60 per cent. In some countries, for example Ghana, Mozambique, Rwanda, Uganda, the proportion of war related civilian deaths has been over 90 per cent.[5] The totals may well exceed those in all the previous centuries of war making. These observations reveal most dramatically the irrelevance of rationally designed methods of conflict resolution to limitation, let alone abolition, of war. The reason for this failure is brought out in the abolitionist philosophy of peace.

It seems that increasingly wars are no longer fought *about* something, such as 'issues' or 'interests' or 'ideologies.' Rather, they are fought because they constitute the *raison d'être* of war as an institution. To see this, consider the above-mentioned parallel between peace research and medical research. Indisputably, dramatic successes of medicine during the last century and a half have been the direct result of uncovering the causes of diseases and developing techniques for removing them. Knowledge of both necessary and sufficient causes is the foundation of scientific medicine. However, from the point of view of immediate application of this knowledge in specific cases, knowledge of necessary causes is more relevant than of sufficient causes. The latter are enormously complex and varied; the former can be pinpointed and hence effectively attacked. The tubercle bacillus is by no means a sufficient cause of tuberculosis (we are probably all carriers). But being an absolutely necessary condition, it is the key to preventing, curing, or controlling the disease: kill the bacillus; prevent its spread.

The same considerations apply to war. Sufficient causes of war are enormously complex and moreover change radically in the course of history. Dynastic wars (so called 'wars of succession'), common in eighteenth century Europe, are no longer thinkable. The same can be said about once-common wars in quest of arable land or slave labour or treasure. The Second World War was widely regarded as an 'ideological war,' just as the Thirty Years' War is often referred to as a 'religious war.' Both interpretations are questionable. In the Thirty Years' War, France, a Catholic country, tended to side with the Protestant powers. In the Second World War, the USSR, a totalitarian state, fought on the side of 'democracies' against Nazi Germany (with which it had been informally allied at the outbreak of the war). In contrast, a necessary condition of war, as we know it, is weapons. Hence general and complete disarmament appears as the most effective way of abolishing war, at least the sort of war that now threatens humanity with extinction. Granted that whether general and complete disarmament is attainable, at least in time to prevent the next and possibly terminal world war, is a moot question. It nevertheless appears to be more promising than either conversion of entire populations to pacifism or institutionalizing arbitration procedures.

The compelling force exerted by war as an institution rather than a consequence of clashing interests of nations, is illustrated by an incident a day or two before the outbreak of hostilities in 1914. For some reason, possibly in response to a frantic appeal by Nicholas II, his cousin, Wilhelm II enquired of Helmuth von Moltke, chief of the general staff, whether it was possible to avert the war by halting mobilization. Moltke is said to have replied that this was out of the question. A troop train was crossing the bridge at Strasbourg every ten minutes. Orders to halt this movement would unleash complete chaos with disastrous effects for Germany. Indeed the meticulous planning of the war had gone on for at least twenty years. To bring the plan down in ruins by a single order must have appeared to Moltke as an act of vandalism like the destruction of a masterpiece. A more recent example of similar mentality was the bombing of Cambodia by Americans on the day before they withdrew from that country after Congress ruled the intervention illegal. The bombing could be justified only by the inadmissibility of letting the unexpended bombs 'go to waste.' It is estimated that 15,000 civilians were killed in that raid.

Evolving Systems

The concept of evolution is much older than its formulation in Darwin's *Origin of Species*, but it has attained its status as the foundation of biological science when, in the light of that work, its teleological ('providential') interpretations were discarded. Beasts of prey were no longer seen as 'provided' with sharp claws and teeth because they had to kill prey to survive; and their prey were no longer seen as possessing swift feet because they had to run to escape the predators. The marvellous and subtle adaptations of living organisms to their environments and ways of life are now seen as consequences of natural selection: those that failed to adapt in the process of evolution (solidly established by overwhelming evidence) are simply no longer with us. Those we see are the end results of a long chain of adaptive changes.

The notion of evolution by adaptation can be extended to 'systems' – entities regarded as generalized organisms. A system in this mode of thinking is any entity that can be recognized as 'itself' in spite of at times radical changes going on within it. Living organisms are 'systems' in this sense, since they are usually recognized as retaining their identity in spite of the fact that their material constituents are being constantly replaced by metabolism. Even some non-material entities satisfy this definition of 'system.' In fact, the 'evolutionary-taxonomic tree' of languages bears a striking resemblance to the corresponding tree of biological taxa, exhibiting analogues of phyla branching into classes, these into families, genera, and so on. The same can be said of the evolutionary courses of artifacts. The 'fossil record' of the motor car, the sewing machine, the howitzer, and the bathing suit can be seen in many museums.

Clearly, institutions can also be regarded as evolving systems. The city of Rome, the Bank of England, the Catholic Church, certain military units, corporations, *etc.* have preserved their 'identities,' some through centuries, in spite of the fact that none of their former human constituents are alive today. Can these surviving entities be regarded as in some way having adapted themselves to a changing environment? The fact that they also 'die' suggests that the surviving ones did. As an example, consider monarchy as a system in this sense. In the nineteenth century, most European states were hereditary monarchies. Some were absolute or near-absolute autocracies, others constitutional monarchies. All four of the former type – the Russian Empire, the German Empire, the Austro-Hungarian Empire and the Turkish Empire 'died,' clearly in consequence of the First World War; all the constitutional monarchies survived. It seems that the latter but not the former turned out to be adapted to a changing political climate.

The dustbin of history is full of defunct institutions: human sacrifice, duelling, chattel slavery, Chinese foot-binding, the Holy Inquisition. From the perspective of the abolitionist philosophy of peace, war appears as an institution which has so far remained virile by adapting itself to changing social environments. The most conspicuous adaptation has been to the massive shift of affect towards war – the change from glorification and romanticization to abhorrence (which points up the dramatic failure of prognoses of the ultimate demise of war, such as those of S. Amos and of the 1911 *Britannica* cited above). However, war, like all institutions can be assumed to be mortal. The abolitionist branch of the peace movement sees its task as that of depriving the institution of war of further opportunities to survive by adaptation and thus ensuring its demise.

Militarism Without Military Tradition

One example of successful adaptation of war to its social environment will suffice to illustrate the process.

The United States never had a military caste as a conspicuous social sector with its own jealously guarded code of honour, publicly displayed presence, heroic traditions and magnificent wardrobes. Nevertheless, in the last half of our century the United States became the most militarized nation on earth in the sense of ubiquitous military presence in industry, politics, and scientific and educational institutions. Characteristic of this presence is the blurred boundary between civilian and military professions. Colin Gray called attention to this peculiarity:

> ... only in the United States is it possible for individuals with relative ease to have 'mixed careers' involving occasional periods of official service, university teaching (or affiliation at least), 'think tank' research, private consulting, possibly employment in the defense industry.[6]

I believe this diffusion of military concerns, modes of thinking, values, *etc.* throughout American society was a result of the way the United States joined the world of chronic warfare in 1917. The stalemate on the Western Front was broken by the massive influx of American material. It was said that the Germans' morale was finally shattered when they saw stores of canned meat in captured trenches during their last offensives in 1918. The American conception of victory, guaranteed by know-how and mass production (rather than valour and dedication), became even clearer when the United States became a belligerent in the Second World War. In this way, war, as it evolved in the twentieth century, became 'adapted' to the principal mainstream preoccupations and values of Americans – technolatry (worship of technology) and business acumen. Witness the following contribution to the problem of allocating funds earmarked for bolstering 'security' in the world of chronic nuclear threat.

> The number and value of enemy targets that can be destroyed (for a given budget) ... takes into account not only the numbers of our offense bombers and missiles but also their operational effectiveness ... It still is, of course, an ambiguous criterion and requires more precise definition. For example, what target systems – population, industry, or military bases – should be used to keep score ...?[7]

Note that in this excerpt there is also an allusion to competitive sports (what should we use to keep score?) – more evidence of the successful adaptation of war to American preoccupations and values.

Implications of the Organismic Conception of War

If war, regarded as an institution, appears as an analogue of a living organism (in the sense of having adapted to its social environment in the course of its evolution), then it seems reasonable to ascribe to it self-preserving strategies, common to all living organisms and their analogues. This conception by no means reflects a tendency towards anthropo-morphism, ascribing consciousness or purposefulness to systems other than human individuals. 'Self-preservation' in this context means no more than the operation of some sort of homeostatic mechanism. Even some inanimate systems seem to exercise 'self-preservation,' for instance by returning to a state of equilibrium following a disturbance. The point is that some form of 'self-preservation' must operate in any system that remains 'itself' during the course of its existence. The institution of war, conceived as a system, is no exception.

Of course, human beings, along with artifacts, think-tanks, arsenals, sources of nourishment (budgets) are among the constituents of the war system. Thus, the efforts of these human components can be directly identified as contributing to the self-preservation of the system. This is what was meant in the beginning of this essay by reference to 'resistance' of the system to the mounting political threats against it. Concrete examples of this resistance are particularly conspicuous in the United States, where intellectuals are clearly recognizable as hawks or doves debating through their respective 'organs' – the former, for example, in *Foreign Affairs*, the latter often in *the Bulletin of the Atomic Scientists*.

Consider the following prognosis by a prominent member of the hawk camp:

> It is safe to predict that strategic studies will enjoy a long and healthy future. Those scholars who believe that, in all save rococo variations, nearly the last important word has been written on issues of interest to strategists, may confidently be proclaimed to be in error.[8]

The author is assuring his readers, among whom, we can assume, are many of his colleagues in the 'defence community' that the war system with its educational and scientific sectors is here to stay and to provide career opportunities and challenges for creative minds. Recall the same author's approving references to 'mixed careers' made possible by the fusion of the corporate, educational and military worlds.

The war system is also widely credited in the United States with ending the debilitating depression of the thirties and with providing a major impetus to the economy since. Witness the protests against closing military bases by communities that have become economically dependent on them. Throughout the Cold War, the war establishments of the two superpowers supported each other by providing an irrefutable *raison d'être* to each other. In this sense they could be more reasonably regarded as allies (cooperating components of the same system) than adversaries. Finally observe how global arms trade keeps the level of global violence high after 'classical' inter-nation wars have apparently become almost obsolete. Most bloodshed now occurs in genocidal intertribal and interethnic wars, in which rival war lords play a major role. Their killing squads provide practically the only 'security' (source of sustenance and a 'meaningful' skilled activity) to the male youth of many Third World countries. This thriving global business derives its support from the global military establishment and, in turn, supports it.

Can the War System Be 'De-legitimized'?

Most interesting is Freeman Dyson's eloquent plea for 'resolving the conflict' between the opponents and the defenders of the war system. In his book, *Weapons and Hope*[9] Dyson pictures humanity as consisting of two 'classes' (as I would call them for want of a better term) – the Warriors and the Victims. Although he does not say so explicitly, he probably thinks of the categories as roles rather than individuals. Thus, in case of a 'final solution' of the human problem the 'warriors' and the 'victims' would become indistinguishable as individuals. Moreover, Dyson presents himself as a member of both 'classes.'

In *Weapons and Hope*, Dyson sets the stage, as it were, for a dialogue between the Warriors and the Victims. Seeing himself in both roles, he is in an excellent position to sketch a meaningful debate. As a clear thinking and feeling human being, he vividly sees the plight of the victims; as a consultant on military technical problems, he is immersed in the world of the warriors. He undertakes two tasks. One is to get the Warriors and the Victims to see each other as human beings rather than as embodiments of wickedness and naiveté respectively. The other is to show that the concerns of both are 'legitimate.' He does well in the first task. His portraits of specific dedicated and humanly attractive Warriors, for example of Robert Oppenheimer and of a German general (acquitted in Nuremberg) are most impressive. But in my opinion he fails in the second task. The concerns of the sincere and humane Warrior can appear legitimate only if war retains its legitimacy as a human enterprise, which in the eyes of the abolitionist it does not. For all practical purposes the International Court of Justice has denied legitimacy both to the use and to the threat of using nuclear weapons. In the eyes of the abolitionist this judgment is a step towards denying legitimacy to war.

The Conversion of Peacemaking into a
New Kind of 'Warmaking'

From the abolitionist's point of view, a reconciliation between Warriors and Victims (regarded as roles, not as individuals) is impossible. Had not the term 'liquidation,' as in 'liquidation of kulaks as a class' been irreparably compromised, I would insist that a principal abolitionist goal ought to be liquidation of the Warrior class, as defined by Freeman Dyson. Respect for persons can be assured by resort to conversion, not of people (assault on their mentality) but of devices and institutions; that is carrying out the 'liquidation' by realizing the twenty-eight centuries old prophesy, 'And they shall beat their swords into ploughshares and their spears into pruning hooks' (Isaiah 2,4). Note that not only conversion of hardware was projected but also of 'software' ('...neither shall they learn war any more'). In modern terms, this would mean the refutation of Colin Gray's prognosis of a 'long and healthy future' for strategic studies.

Isaiah's position, as reflected in these remarks, was rather that of a pacifist than of an abolitionist. They seem to have been based on the assumption that disarmament would be a consequence of expelling predilections to violence from the human psyche rather than the other way around. Actually, cause and effect in this context are most likely interchangeable (linked by feedback). The abolitionist's insistence on the primacy of disarmament over purging the human psyche is based on practical considerations: resistance to disarmament is more likely to yield to political pressure than aggressive urges or acquisitiveness or power addiction to reminders of moral imperatives.

Turning to peacemaking, we find that is has been often motivated by perception of a common enemy. For example, the efforts of both Vladimir Monomach and of King George of Bohemia were directed essentially to preparation of war – against the plundering Polovtzy in tenth-century Russia, against the invading Turks in fifteenth-century Europe. This is especially true of consolidation of political units. Clans were consolidated into tribes to fight against hostile tribes; tribes into states, states into alliances to take defensive or offensive action against rival tribes, states, or blocs. Thus internal pacification went hand in hand with exacerbation of violence against external enemies often created by these very consolidations or alliances. The net result was an increase rather than a reduction of the total volume and intensity of violence.

The apparent incompatibility of 'irreconcilable conflict between Warriors and Victims' or 'war against war' with peace advocacy disappears if the struggle is seen as one not against a human enemy. In the context of abolition, this means, essentially, that no one is to be disadvantaged by the consequences of dismantling the institutions comprising the war system. The elimination of military units, entire industries, entire educational institutions, entire professions must be accompanied by creation of suitable substitutes. Replacements must be found for every eliminated job, project and institute. It is unlikely that costs of replacements will exceed the savings from cancelled military spending, certainly not in the long run and most certainly not the cost of future wars.

Further, if the sociobiologists are right, that is, if pugnacity is actually genetically embedded in human nature (carried over from the times when it was adaptive), a 'war against war' can be a way of utilizing this aggressiveness for constructive purposes. One can be dedicated to a 'struggle,' derive satisfaction from 'victories,' savour orgies of destruction (of lethal devices), mobilize ingenuity to invent more effective or safer methods of making devices that are *at best* useless *actually* useless.

In this struggle, every success makes further successes more likely, regardless of its relative importance with regard to reducing the overall threat to humanity. Consider the success of the anti-landmine campaign. In themselves, repugnant as they are because of the predominance of the helpless and harmless among their victims, landmines account for a minuscule fraction of those killed or likely to be killed or crippled by war technology. The importance of the widely publicized 'victory' over landmines was in its role as a powerful stimulus to further efforts. The search for the next target, the planning for a campaign against it, the campaign itself, the lessons learned from its strengths and weaknesses – all these consequences can be expected to contribute to the morale and effectiveness of the abolitionist movement.

Clearly a victory over nuclear weapons will be a decisive turning point in the 'war against war.' A 'victory' in this context would be marked by a commitment of nuclear nations (declared and undeclared) to a time table for the implementation of the 'final solution' of the nuclear dilemma rather than of the human race. In fact, the newly concocted argument against total nuclear disarmament, namely, the necessity of retaliating against a chemical or biological attack by 'rogue states,' looks suspiciously like a further adaptation of the omnicidal system to an increasingly hostile social environment. A victory against nuclear weapons would carry with it a demolition of the standard arguments of the Warriors to the effect that deterrence or balance of power contribute to the preservation of peace. In short, victories in a 'war against war' would inadvertently have ideological side effects – changes in ways of thinking that Einstein once regarded as indispensable for the survival of humanity.

References

1. C.H.M. Yarrow, *Quaker Experiences in International Reconciliation*, New Haven: Yale University Press, 1978.
2. P. Dickson, *Think Tanks*, New York: Atheneum, 1971.
3. S. Amos, *Political and Legal Remedies for War*, London: Cassell, Potter, Galpin & Co., 1880, pp. 6-7.
4. *ibid.*, pp. 15-16.
5. R.L. Sivard, *World Military and Social Expenditures*, Washington: World Priorities, 1996.
6. C. Gray, *Strategic Studies and Public Policy*, Lexington: The University of Kentucky Press, 1982.
7. 'The Criterion Problem,' C.J. Hitch and R.N. McKean, in *American National Security*, M. Berkowitz and P.G. Bock eds., New York: The Free Press, 1965.
8. Gray, 1982, *op.cit.,* p. 7.
9. F. Dyson, *Weapons and Hope*, New York: Harper and Row, 1984.

11

The Abolition of War: Realistic Utopianism

Bruce Kent

The culture of war was as much part of my upbringing as going to church, cleaning my teeth and going to bed when told to. I still remember as a small boy looking at my father's wounded leg with fascination. A shell landed close to him in 1917, and every once in a while some tiny piece of shrapnel would work its way to the surface of an injury that never really healed. November 11th was a day to remember as all of London ground to a halt and the guns could be heard booming from Hyde Park. My cigarette card collection of the regiments of the Empire was a special treasure. In those pre-war years I never remember even a mention, at home or at school, of the League of Nations.

At boarding school later, no less than eight portraits of Old Boys who had won the Victoria Cross looked down on us at mealtimes. The cadet corps was as normal a part of life as sports day or the Christmas play. The Second World War was a bit of an adventure, with searchlights and guns on Hampstead Heath, and air-raid wardens checking on blackout. Leaving school to go into the army was what everyone did. Conscientious objectors were people who got white feathers, or at least deserved them. The first meeting of the United Nations General Assembly took place in London while I was still at school. I do not remember any mention of that event.

My first personal experience of a war in which I saw people getting killed was during the Nigerian civil war of 1966-1970. It was a war which employed a highly indiscriminate traditional weapon: mass starvation. It was a war which at last made me start thinking about alternatives.

Since those days, by a thousand different steps, I have come to the conviction that war and militarism are not inevitable consequences of the human condition. On the contrary, despite the grip that militarism has on our society, I believe that the time has come to say that whatever happened in the past we have now to build a culture of peace if we are to survive at all.

After many long years of doing just that, it now seems to me that it is not enough to protest about specific weapons systems, valuable though such protest is, and successful as it sometimes has been. The time has come to challenge the belief, held by so many, that war and the preparations for war are an unfortunate necessity and in the real world the only road to genuine security.

Two people in particular have helped me to change my thinking. The first was Barbara Ward, later Lady Jackson, a distinguished Christian economist who died too young. Always a solid rock of common sense, in a 1972 speech to a meeting of non-governmental groups in Geneva, she made her practical ideas clear to me. Hers was not a demand for instant pacifism with lions and lambs happily munching together. It was a step-by-step approach. Why, she asked, was it normal for conflict to be resolved, for the most part non-violently, within the nation state framework, while violent solutions had such a high priority in the resolution of international conflict?

She urged people to think about the structures of peace that are missing at the international level. She talked about courts, legal systems and police forces. She stressed that while within the state framework the sale of weapons, if not forbidden was rigidly controlled, the export of weapons was thought to be a normal part of the international economy. Within states and lesser communities all kinds of mediation and conflict prevention mechanisms are in place. Between states such mechanisms are largely lacking. She did not idealize the situation. Violence is not unknown within states and non-violent conflict resolution has also been successful on the world stage. It would be quite unjust to the International Court of Justice to suggest otherwise.

Her great gift as a realistic utopian was to stimulate imagination and to make people ask questions. Most of all she wanted to know why the boundaries of non-violent conflict resolution should not be extended. She was the kind of person George Bernard Shaw had in mind when he wrote 'Some people see things as they are and ask 'Why?' I dream things that never were and ask 'Why not?''

Barbara Ward belonged to the same family of realistic utopians as Joseph Rotblat, the second source of my inspiration. His energy and determination would be impressive in a man of forty, let alone one of ninety. Reading his Nobel lecture, given in Oslo on December 10, 1995, was an enormous encouragement. It contained a passionate appeal to scientists to redirect their skills to the development of a world of peace and not of war. He repeated the 1995 appeal from Professor Hans Bethe, one-time director of the Theoretical Division of Los Alamos, who said:

> I call on all scientists in all countries to cease and desist from work creating, developing, improving and manufacturing further nuclear weapons, and for that matter other weapons of potential mass destruction, such as chemical and biological weapons.

In the last part of his speech Professor Rotblat went beyond the repudiation of particular weapons. 'War,' he said, 'must cease to be an admissible social institution. We must learn to resolve our disputes by means other than military confrontation.' He then met head-on the accusation that a war-free world was just a utopian dream. 'It is not utopian. There already exist in the world large regions, for example the European Union, within which war is inconceivable. What is needed is to extend these to cover the world's major powers...'

Joseph Rotblat and Barbara Ward speak the same language. It is not of course a new language. Turning swords into ploughshares and studying the elimination of war are themes with ancient pedigrees. The vision has always been there. It has recently had some contemporary re-statements. In 1945 the Red Cross said that 'War, which remains an anomaly in a civilized world, has taken on so devastating and universal a character ... that every thought and every effort should be aimed, above all, at making it impossible.' The preamble to the Charter of the United Nations itself declared that the people of the world are 'determined to save succeeding generations from the scourge of war ...' UNESCO's 1989 Statement on Violence rejected the notion that wars are inevitable. 'The same species who invented war is capable of inventing peace. The responsibility lies with each one of us.' The stress on personal responsibility is more than welcome at a time when few are prepared to accept it. We are both responsible for what we do and for what we allow to happen.

All these ideas are not just fine words and noble dreams, though they represent an enormous challenge. About thirty wars, nearly all within rather than between states, are in progress at the moment. Wars have killed at least twenty million people since 1945. Globally we still spend some $700 billion a year on what we now call defence – a sum almost a hundred times greater than that which we spend on all the work of the United Nations and its agencies.

The environmental consequences of militarism are profound, though they are often left out of the equation when governments meet to discuss such matters. The Rio conference of 1992 deliberately excluded militarism from its agenda though it is one of the greatest causes both of global poverty and environmental degradation. Yet Mostafa Tolba, Director of the United Nations Environmental Programme, said before that conference began, 'Disarmament and other security issues are not on the agenda, but global discussions and international agreements [on development and the environment] are worthless without progress on these issues.'

So how to make progress? It is easy to list what we lack. We still lack, despite hopeful developments, a world criminal court with jurisdiction over individuals and states. We do not have a system for controlling, let alone ending, the world trade in weapons, though the United Nations register of certain larger systems is a step in the right direction. Many major industrial powers still look on arms exports as an essential part of their economy. We lack an effective pre-crisis international monitoring system.

We lack the international machinery which might encourage the poor of the world to believe that there are roads other than violence that might lead to economic justice. No international legislation exists to define as criminal work undertaken by scientists on weapons of mass destruction. No international reward, respect or protection is given to those, like Mordechai Vanunu, who repudiate state secrecy in the interest of global security. We have no world police force of the kind envisaged by article 43 of the UN Charter.

Perhaps one of the most serious global deficiencies lies in the lack of recognition which would give political voice to those denied one by the sovereign state basis of the UN Charter. 'Nothing,' says article 2.7 of the Charter, 'shall authorize the United Nations to intervene in matters which are essentially within the domestic jurisdiction of any state.' Since the wars of today are in the main civil wars, the sovereign state limitations of the present Charter are all too obvious. For instance if the 30 million Kurds who live in at least four different countries have no voice and no status, how are they to be persuaded that war is not the only answer to oppression?

The Russell-Einstein manifesto was clear on this point. 'The abolition of war will demand distasteful limitations of national sovereignty.' Distasteful to whom? Certainly to those who think that the world can be divided into autonomous sovereign separate boxes. But not distasteful at all to those who know perfectly well that there is today no absolute sovereignty in questions of security, economics, health, pollution, population or human rights.

Happily there is a new globalism in the air, thanks especially to the work of many citizens' organizations ranging alphabetically from Amnesty

International to the World Development Movement. These new globalists are not lacking in love of country or culture. But they know well that the political structures that emerged from nineteenth century nationalism cannot represent the last word in human organization. In too many ways the growth of an ever more interdependent world means that claims of national sovereignty are just not adequate. The challenge is to build the international structures within which international problems, and war is one of the greatest, can be resolved.

The problems are great. Those who wish to abolish war have to overcome a culture of militarism that has lasted for centuries. It is a culture that finds its expression in many different institutions. Churches too often have close military links. Their forms of worship are often expressed in terms of conflict, violence and victory. Military cadet corps are normal adjuncts to many of the elite Church schools. Military chaplains, paid for by the state, give a legitimacy to military structures and concepts. Non-violent solutions to international conflict seem unrealistic by comparison.

The same problems arise with many universities and other academic institutions. Ministry of Defence research grants are eagerly sought. Research scientists do not often bite the hand that feeds them. Trade unions, too, easily absorb military perceptions. Lacking properly-funded government arms conversion agencies, peace movement challenges to military production are seen as imperilling jobs. Non-governmental organizations enjoying legal charitable status and the financial benefits which result from that status, hesitate to become involved in what might be judged to be political activity. Challenges to national militarism will certainly be so defined.

The militarism of the media is all too clear. It is expressed, for instance, by conformity to militarist thinking in the management of news. For the decade of the 1980s news commentators regularly explained the need for yet more nuclear weapons on the grounds of 'imbalances' that had supposedly to be corrected. This at a time when both superpowers were perfectly capable of destroying civilized life on the planet with but a fraction of their nuclear stockpiles. It was the media also that helped to turn the word 'unilateral' into a term of contempt even though it was precisely through a series of unilateral actions that Gorbachev did so much to bring the Cold War to an end.

The militarism of the media also expresses itself through its regular diet of violent entertainment and war glorification. The Second World War never seems to have come to an end. As I write the BBC has provided us with yet another range of war films for our Christmas entertainment. The legless hero, Douglas Bader, flew again, and Mrs

Miniver once more faced the Germans with her brave and gentle smile. Children's comic TV cartoons are dotted with evil monsters, eventually destroyed by brave people fighting for justice as they outwit the ray-guns of their wicked opponents.

Ten years ago a national newspaper surveyed pre-9 p.m. television on the four main channels for one week. They counted 131 murders, 22 shootings, 21 assaults, 10 bombings and 13 riots. Yet, despite that weekly dose of horror we expect children to grow up with constructive ideas about non-violent conflict resolution.

In short, any campaign aimed at the abolition of war has to recognize both the size of the challenge and also the excellent work already being done by many different organizations on aspects of the problem.

The term 'peace movement' has surely to be redefined. It was never meant to be an exclusive label. All human beings are endowed with a sense of justice and a yearning to live in peace. There are certainly some people whose minds are so distorted that they feed on cruelty and violence. Militarism, however, does not depend on such people. It exists because for many decent people who have no love of killing, war, as they see it, is in the last resort the only option left open. For such people Barbara Ward had these words:

> We have, therefore to insist that far from disarmament being unusual and impossible, it is the normal state of civilized people inside their own community. To say that we are not capable of this is simple nonsense. Most of the time this is actually what we do.

There is a millennium mood in the air that owes little to new domes and strange yet-to-be-revealed but certainly expensive experiences. There is today a yearning for a world in which we and our five-and-a-half billion fellow residents can live together in peace, justice and order. Utopias do not arrive pre-packaged, and there will be many steps on the road that leads in that direction. Joseph Rotblat, to whom these essays are dedicated, has already earned our respect for his courage and persistence. But now he has also our admiration for raising our sights to this inspiring objective and for encouraging us to take our own steps in that direction.

Perhaps Tennyson was casting a Rotblat-like forward shadow in his *In Memoriam* when he wrote:

> Ring out the narrowing lust of gold.
> Ring out the thousand wars of old.
> Ring in the thousand years of peace.

12

The 'Moral Equivalent of War'

Sissela Bok

The war against war is going to be no holiday excursion or camping party. The military feelings are too deeply grounded to abdicate their place among our ideals until better substitutes are offered than the glory and shame that come to nations as well as individuals from the ups and downs of politics and the vicissitudes of trade... So long as the anti-militarists propose no substitutes for the disciplinary function of war, no *moral equivalent* of war, analogous, one might say, to the mechanical equivalent of heat, so long they fail to realize the full inwardness of the situation.

William James, 'The Moral Equivalent of War'[1]

In 1910, as the world's great powers were gearing up for a war with unprecedented destructive potential, the philosopher and psychologist William James set forth his proposals for a re-energized 'war on war.'[2] Merely exposing war's evils, he held, and warning of its tendency to brutalize and corrupt participants, would do little to still the waves of passion engulfing societies moving towards military confrontation. What was needed, rather, was to rechannel for constructive rather than warlike needs the energies, the sense of honour, the discipline and the loyalties that the most effective armies engender.

Admittedly, James conceded, the prospect of such rechannelling on the scale needed was at the time only an infinitely remote utopia; but in the long run, and with leaders capable of seizing historic opportunities, he had no doubt that 'the ordinary prides and shames of social man' could organize such a constructive replacement for war.[3] Now that we near the end of a century marked as no other by murderous mass wars, when societies struggle to adjust to a post-Cold War world with fewer immediate threats of vast conflagration but more desperate and vicious civil wars than ever, we have special reason to look to James' proposals. Must we still think of them as utopian? If not, how can they be implemented on the scale now needed? And what can we learn from his probing of the psychological forces that drive groups to engage even in mutually suicidal wars?

I take James to have used the word 'moral' in two senses, as he called for a moral equivalent to war. The first sense is that of the equivalent being more ethical, both from the point of view of the goals sought and the means used in too many wars. To serve the goals of peace, national survival and thriving, when pared of the elements of revenge and destruction and conquest fueling many wars, societies could draw on many of the same virtues stressed in the conduct of war – fidelity, cohesiveness, tenacity, heroism, inventiveness, courage and strength.

The second sense of 'moral' for James is that of the 'psychological' as opposed to the 'physical' – a contrast common in French and German philosophy at the time. As soon as one considers the persuasiveness and not merely the strength or validity of arguments, their psychological impact becomes crucial. It is then not enough for opponents of war to stress the immorality or the self-defeating quality of war, or even to demonstrate that the virtues of war are capable of being enlisted for peaceful purposes. The psychological aspects of war must be taken into account as well, and channelled towards constructive goals: the bonding and comradeship that war engenders, the risk-taking, the sense of self-sacrifice for the sake of a purpose larger than oneself, and the sheer thrill that war can generate. Above all, it is useless to attempt to dissuade those who love war by pointing to its expense or its horror: 'The horror makes the thrill.'[4]

Neither overpowering ethical reasoning nor sheer psychological advocacy could suffice, then, for an equivalent of war to be moral, in James' sense. Whatever equivalent is proposed, it must be moral in both the ethical and the psychological senses of the word to stand a chance of having an impact on the currents in human history that appear to lead relentlessly towards collective bloodshed.

As for that equivalent of war in its own right, a final state of 'peace' was not the equivalent that James had in mind. The word 'equivalent' comes from the Latin 'equi,' meaning 'equal,' and 'valere,' meaning 'being strong.' The equivalent to war that James envisaged had to be of equal strength in achieving societal goals.

For this reason, the moral equivalent to war had to be a *process*, an engagement of human activities for constructive and peaceful purposes, rather than some elusive state of lasting peace that could only be envisaged as the end result of such a process. To be equivalent to war, this process, so long as it is moral, and thus precisely not destructive or exploitative in the manner of war, must be at least equal to it in its felt value and significance for societies. It must, like war, rely on co-operation at every level, and captivate psychologically through its confrontation of danger, its call for discipline, its opportunities for fellowship, sacrifice and even heroism.

While James did not see violence as bound to beleaguer human societies forever, he acknowledged that many people glory in war on account of the passions and loyalties it arouses, and the determination and discipline with which, at best, it can be pursued. What has since become clear, especially in social scientific studies of post-traumatic stress disorder done after the Second World War, and especially after the Vietnam War, is that a certain number of combatants develop an erotic attachment to violence. They come to love killing. After they return home from war, a proportion of veterans find that nothing else can engage them as war once did. The more cruel the means of combat that have been employed, and the greater the human suffering produced, the more difficult it becomes for those who became inured to inflicting it to readjust. For their sakes as well as for that of their victims, James' question of how to provide an equivalent to war that does not wreak such psychological havoc is more pertinent than ever.

What James proposed, keeping these psychological proclivities in mind, as he saw nations arming and escalating their martial rhetoric during the decade before the First World War, was something akin to what we would now call a domestic peace corps. He suggested that nations draft young people to serve the constructive needs of their country – joining winter fishing fleets, for example, or working at road building or tunnel making. If rightly organized, such activities could challenge and rechannel those energies and enthusiasms that pour forth so easily in war, this time for peaceful purposes.

Even as James acknowledged that such a proposal would have to seem utopian at first, events have proved him right in holding that it would be capable of implementation some day. By now, a number of societies are drafting or otherwise engaging young people for such purposes. Much more has been done than even he could imagine to engage both men and women, old as well as well as young of all nationalities, to serve across the world to work at tasks more ambitious than those James mentioned. These include service in the many national and international organizations now engaged in teaching, human rights work, humanitarian assistance, and peacekeeping.

Eighteen years after James' article appeared, Walter Lippmann, once James' student at Harvard University, suggested that a moral equivalent to war was surely necessary but far from sufficient. In an article entitled 'The

Political Equivalent of War,' Lippmann suggested, as James would probably have agreed had he lived to experience the First World War, that both sides in many conflicts do believe themselves to be acting morally in the face of an adversary bent on their destruction. On the eve of war, he writes, nations

> almost invariably feel that they are innocent householders who are about to be invaded by robbers, or that they are witnesses to some dastardly outrage which is about to be perpetrated on their neighbors. The choice as it presents itself is not between the crime of war and the righteousness of peace, but between ruin and disgrace on the one hand, and self-preservation, courage, and honor on the other.

At such times of crisis, stronger preventive mechanisms are clearly needed than engaging citizens in constructive work at home or abroad. Similarly, more immediate and far-reaching efforts are needed to restore the rule of law and the respect for human rights in societies ravaged by war.

In proposing how to meet such crises, Lippmann could draw on his experience of the First World War and its chaotic aftermath, to urge that 'It is not sufficient to propose an equivalent for the military virtues. It is even more important to work out an equivalent for the military methods and objectives.'[5] Otherwise it will be impossible for the international community to bring about a transition from war to peace, from chaos to order, and from revolution to the rule of law. Lippmann used the examples of the US and other civil wars and of the arduous process of re-establishing the rule of law after such societal upheavals, to propose that international society needed similar networks of institutions, and would continue to be at the mercy of forces leading to war so long as these were lacking:

> [S]urely the history of the establishment of peace in civil societies goes to show that any genuine political equivalent of violence must comprise a vast network of legislative, judicial, executive, social, and cultural institutions. Is there any reason to suppose that international peace is any easier to attain than domestic peace?[6]

Just as we have now come much farther than James could have foreseen in providing opportunities for the long-range constructive work for peace that he proposed, so we have witnessed the gradual creation and strengthening of international institutions such as those advocated by Lippmann. Both developments, however, have taken place in a context of warfare of a scope that James, unlike Lippmann, could have had no reason to imagine possible.

Far more is needed on both scores if the international community is to deal with today's wars. By now, even as the threat of all-out nuclear conflagration has receded, the number of civil wars and of resulting complex humanitarian emergencies of a most intractable nature has continued to grow. While many more individuals and societal groups are engaged in efforts both towards a moral and a political equivalent to war, many others are equally determinedly at work to promote war, not peace.

Those who founded Pugwash laboured to bring to an end a situation so potentially violent that it threatened the survival of all humanity. Now that their work, along with that of so many others, has helped defuse the balance of terror with which we lived for so long, we have come upon a paradox: just as we can breathe more easily regarding the prospects of collective nuclear annihilation, so many more localized communities the world over are now newly rent by utterly self-destructive hatreds, reducing to rubble what were once thriving villages and cities, digging graves for ever more of their fellow citizens. And everywhere, we see civilians victimized as rarely before: four decades ago, the proportion of civilians among war-related casualties was already grotesquely high, at 50 per cent; by now it has reached an unimaginable 90 per cent.[7]

A few years ago, some spoke grandiosely of a New World Order as being at hand. Even then, most of us may have seen little evidence of such a new order. But we did think that the time had come when a tremendous concentration of collective effort might at last be possible; we did think that societies would now at least have the opportunity to address more energetically the vast problems they face collectively, such as those posed by epidemics, famines, and environmental deterioration of every kind. And we surely thought that there was not a moment to lose before moving ahead.

Instead, one opportunity after another for such collective action has gone for naught. The ethnic warfare, the slaughter and torture and rape that we witness in so many regions, have stunned the world community. And I use the word 'stunned' advisedly. The extent of these barbaric practices, and the ease with which apparently civilized communities become engulfed in them, have astounded and horrified us. But too often they have also overwhelmed, stupefied, and dazed many in the world community, bringing bewilderment about how to respond, and a sense of impotence and great discouragement.

Everyone recognizes that such conflicts can leap across frontiers and multiply many times over. Few imagine that military intervention on the vast scale that all existing conflicts, let alone all future ones, would require, is the right answer or even a possible one. The peacekeeping, peacemaking, and conflict resolution efforts discussed in Pugwash working groups can do only so much in the Bosnias and Rwandas of this world. There are far greater prospects for prevention of similar conflicts before they have raged out of control; but such prevention, too, takes a level of organization and of will that are now lacking, and promises to devour scarce resources that could have gone to alleviate so many other pressing human problems.

It will matter, for purposes of such efforts at redirection and re-engagement for peace, to draw on the extraordinary tradition of non-violent resistance that this century has known – in part as a response to the levels of violence: a tradition developed by Gandhi, Martin Luther King, and those who stood for people's power in the Philippines and Solidarity in Poland; and a tradition explored and developed now by persons like Vaclav Havel and Adam Michnik.

One of the legacies of Gandhi matters to us especially in this context. It is the example he set of someone deeply rooted in his own cultural and religious heritage who still remains utterly opposed to all forms of social, ethnic or religious intolerance.   Evil means, he insisted, corrupt and degrade not only the purposes for which they are undertaken but also the persons who stoop to such means. Overcoming the urge to resort to such means is hardest when one aims to rectify past injustices. It is because 'Hate the sin and not the sinner,' is a precept so rarely practised that 'the poison of hatred spreads in the world.'[8]

These movements elicited, at their best, just what William James had in mind: both a moral and a psychological equivalent of war. They involved, as well, the development of the institutional networks for which Lippmann called. But what still remains in question is: how can we shift much more massively in that direction? How can we move sufficiently energetically to be able to cope with collective problems of a magnitude that neither James nor Lippmann could have foreseen?

References

1.   William James, 'The Moral Equivalent of War,' in *The Works of William James: Essays in Religion and Morality*, ed. Frederick Burckhardt, Harvard University Press, 1982, pp. 162 and 169.
2.   I draw, in this essay, on Sissela Bok, 'A Moral Equivalent of War,' in *A World at the Crossroads: New Conflicts, New Solutions*, ed. Joseph Rotblat and Sven Hellman, Singapore: World Scientific, pp.86-92; Sissela Bok, *A Strategy for Peace*, New York: Vintage Press, 1991; and Sissela Bok, *Common Values*, University of Missouri Press, 1996.
3.   *Ibid.,* p. 172.
4.   *Ibid.,* p. 168.

5. Walter Lippmann, 'The Political Equivalent of War,' *Atlantic Monthly*, v. 142, August 1928, p. 181.
6. *Ibid.*, p. 187.
7. Michael Renner, *Critical Juncture: The Future of Peacekeeping*, Worldwatch Paper 113, Worldwatch Institute, 1993, p. 9.
8. Mohandas Gandhi, *Autobiography*, Boston: Beacon Press, 1993, p. 276.

13

The United Nations and Peacekeeping

John C. Polanyi

Nobody needs to be reminded that life is fraught with peril. That is unlikely to change. We do not seek to create heaven on earth but to find a direction that, over ensuing generations, will offer hope for mankind. It is in that spirit that we approach the unique institution that we call the United Nations, and also the important aspect of its activities that we have come to know as Peacekeeping.

There is no doubt as to the central purpose of the United Nations; it was born out of war to prevent war. The horrors of the First World War had led directly to the founding of the League of Nations in 1919, the year following the end of the war. The still greater suffering, this time both military and civilian, in the Second World War, led to the establishment of the United Nations in 1945, the year that the European war ended.

The death toll in the Second World War was 40 million, as compared with 20 million dead in the First World War; a vastly greater slaughter following one of already inconceivable dimensions. And the slaughter in the second conflict was markedly greater as a fraction of the world's population; 1.7% of the world's people perished in the Second World War as against 1.1% in the First World War (all figures from the World Bank).

But 1945 marked more than the ending of the Second World War, the world's bloodiest conflict. The year of the founding of the UN coincided with the advent of weapons that promised worse in the future. These weapons when introduced were one thousand times more destructive than conventional high explosives. And shortly thereafter, the power of nuclear weapons increased to one million times the destructiveness of the conventional weapons of the Second World War.

As a consequence, it appeared to many of the founders of the UN that war had reached its apotheosis, having become nothing less than an agent for suicide. An effective instrument of global governance seemed to be

133

not merely a civilized option, as in the case of the League, but the only option. It would not be possible to wait until after a Third World War in order to establish a world body to deal with war.

Nor was there any real doubt as to why the previous attempt, the League of Nations, had failed. It had failed quite simply because of lack of conviction that it was needed. Major nations – such as the United States, which had laid the basis of the League – refused to join it since, on reflection, they were unwilling to restrict their freedom of action to the extent that a global alliance required. Other major nations – Japan, Italy, Germany, Russia – joined, but subsequently failed to abide by their undertaking to refrain from unilateral military action. Given this widespread lack of commitment, it was to be expected that the League would fail.

The League of Nations was committed to a policy of 'collective security,' as is the United Nations today. Its members had agreed to combat aggression, 'collectively.' It is through a similar commitment to collective security that we attempt to keep peace within a state. The criminal is put on notice that infractions of the law will be countered by collective action of the citizenry. The case of John Smith, apprehended for commission of a crime, is listed in court documents as 'John Smith versus the state,' not John Smith versus the crime's victim. The collective combines unmatched authority with unrivalled power, consequently it assumes responsibility for the protection of all.

Collective security works. But only if the collective supports it. The collective of the League failed in this when Japan invaded China. It failed once more when Italy invaded Ethiopia. Thereupon collective security, having lost faith in itself, collapsed. And not coincidentally, the Second World War ensued.

The League passed away but not the need for it. That need became more acute not only because weapons became more fearful, but because war became more total. The 'enemy,' over the years from 1935-1945, gradually came to be re-defined to include every man, woman and child and every asset on the opposing side. This new ethic having opened the way to mass destruction, new technology proceeded to make it feasible. The tools of war were extended from nuclear weapons to a broad array of instruments, including chemical and biological weapons, deliverable virtually instantaneously anywhere in the world.

And so, on June 26, 1945 in San Francisco, there was signed the Charter of the United Nations, the most important document in the history of legislation since the signing of the Magna Carta in 1215. That document of seven centuries ago had given the citizens of England powerful rights in the face of the authority of the King. In comparable fashion the UN Charter challenged the divine right of the state to act as it pleased in respect of citizens abroad or at home.

'We, the peoples of the United Nations,' the Charter begins, directing the eyes of the world away from the state to those who comprise it,... 'We, the peoples ... determined to save succeeding generations from the scourge of war, which twice in our lifetimes has brought untold sorrow to mankind, and to reaffirm faith in fundamental human rights [and] in the dignity and worth of the human person... undertake as follows.'

This invocation opened the door to collective action in respect not only to conflicts between states, but also within the borders of a state; not merely inter-state but also intra-state. Both morality and practicality required this. Morality because one cannot regard as acceptable within states the very types of abuse that one condemns between states. Practicality, since aggression by one faction against another within a state is highly likely to lead to intervention on behalf of aggrieved parties by their friends abroad; it is a natural progression from intra-state violence to inter-state. Fire spreads.

Following its preamble the Charter launches into a declaration of Purposes and Principles beginning at Chapter I, Article 1, of which I quote paragraph 1: The purpose of the United Nations, we are told, is, 'To maintain international peace and security, and to that end: to take effective collective measures for the prevention and removal of threats to the peace...' Under 'Principles' (Article 21, paragraph 5) it is then agreed that 'All Members shall give the United Nations every assistance in any action it takes in accordance with the present Charter, and shall refrain from giving assistance to any state against which the United Nations is taking preventive or enforcement action.'

This early reference to the need for enforcement, should peaceful means of persuasion fail, is underscored later in the Charter. Should other measures to obtain compliance seem inadequate the UN (I quote from Chapter VII, Article 42) 'may take such action by air, sea or land forces as may be necessary to maintain or restore international peace and security.' To round out this picture it should be noted that it is explicitly stated in the Charter that any of these measures required for the maintenance of peace, including force, can be applied equally to states that are not members of the UN.

The collective was to have an authority that exceeded that of any state on earth which might wish to go its separate way (see Chapter I, Article 2, paragraph 6). Similarly, within a state we deny the criminal the option of rejecting the law of the land, since, were that a possibility, all criminals would avail themselves of it and laws would have no force.

This preamble leads me to three questions, which I propose to address in turn.   First, does the law of the land have its counterpart internationally? Second, can states, or individuals, be induced to support international law as, in large measure, they support domestic law, and as the UN Charter commits them to support international law?   (By 'international law' I mean a higher law than that of any individual state; thus international law may decree behaviour between states or within states – it is the source of authority that supersedes national authority. More on this later.) Third, and finally, supposing that the answer to questions one and two is in the affirmative, by what means should we seek to enforce the law internationally?

In decades past, realists raised their eyebrows at the mention of international 'law.' Today one sees fewer such raised eyebrows as even the realists become aware of our increasing dependence on international regulation. In today's world rich and poor centre their hopes for a better life on international trade, openness to foreign investment, convertible currencies, and membership in international economic partnerships. None of this is possible, they realise, in the absence of rules of conduct to be found, for example, in the statutes of the International Monetary Fund, the World Bank, and the World Trade Organization, to say nothing of a network of only slightly less sweeping agreements and organizations.

This globalized market place, based upon the freedom to own, to travel and trade, has led, in one country after another, to more open debate and participatory government, creating pressure for democracy. This in turn, has supported the rule of law, since what is arbitrary and unjust has become visible and subject to challenge.

The transfer of power from rulers to ruled that we term 'democracy' has moderated political adventurism abroad. As a consequence today's world is marked by a prevalence of intra-state (internal) conflicts, rather than the inter-state conflicts of the past. This change has occurred since the fall of the Berlin wall in 1989 and the attendant collapse of the USSR.

Though we are all conscious of the continuing horrors of these intra-state conflicts, most recently in Somalia, Rwanda and the former Yugoslavia, we should be aware, and profoundly grateful, that the decline of wars in which one state is pitted against another has resulted in the saving of millions of lives. If we are unwilling to acknowledge that it is better to have smaller tragedies than larger ones, then we lose our compass and are prevented from building a better world. Excessive despair gives the appearance of sensitivity, but is in fact an act of betrayal on the part of the constituency we need most – those who care.

I began by asking whether there exists an international counterpart to domestic law as is presupposed in the UN Charter's call for 'collective security' as an instrument to halt aggression. I end by saying that, as a result of a variety of influences that technology has brought to the modern world, the prohibition of inter-state aggression is stronger than ever before in history. Not so strong as to invite complacency, but strong enough to raise the question why it is that the prohibition against intra-state violence remains so weak.

We began by looking for a counterpart to domestic laws internationally, and we end by looking for a counterpart to international laws domestically. We are on the threshold of a world where collective security arrangements, uncertain though they may be, are often sufficiently strong to deter a government from international adventures, but insufficient to deter factions at home from lethal adventurism.

This leads to my second question. If internationally recognized norms for the behaviour of states do in fact exist, as I have claimed that they increasingly do, is there willingness to enforce these norms? The answer, as I have just suggested, is different in respect of inter-state and intra-state relations.

This is not surprising. The new-thinking that led first to the establishment of the League of Nations and then to the founding of the UN, represented a revolution in that it challenged the right of sovereign states to declare war on one another. Its focus, however, was inter-state behaviour. According to the Charter war was restricted to self-defence, and even then was to be a collective rather than a unilateral undertaking.

In the realm of intra-state prohibitions the Charter was deliberately ambiguous. It spoke, it is true, on behalf of 'peoples' (not states), and it affirmed faith in human rights and the individual's worth, but it stopped short of claiming the right to enforce respect for such supposedly 'internal' matters.

However, it did leave the door ajar. All 'threats to the peace,' it proclaimed, are a proper matter for UN action, up to the extreme of UN enforcement. It was for the Security Council to determine what constituted such a 'threat to the peace.' Happily, in recent years the Security Council has taken the step of identifying the gross abuse of human rights within states as constituting 'threats to peace.'

So long as the world was locked in the frozen embrace of the Cold War, little progress was possible towards this extension of the definition of threats to the peace. However, the pressure was building to acknowledge that internal lawlessness on the part of a state was incompatible with an external devotion to law, and that arbitrary arrests and killings at home presented a threat to peace and security abroad.

When Mr. Gorbachev said precisely that, over a decade ago, in launching his courageous campaign on behalf of legality in the Soviet Union, he was speaking not only for himself but for a wide constituency. The door which

I referred to as being ajar, the door to the recognition of internal barbarism as a proper concern of the UN, then opened further.

Since 1988 the majority of UN operations have been directed at intra-state conflicts (see Boutros Ghali, *Supplement to An Agenda for Peace*, 1995). Prior to that date only one in five interventions related to intra-state conflict. (This reflects the fact that, according to UN figures, of the over eighty conflicts that have broken out around the world since the fall of the Berlin Wall, only three have been inter-state, the great majority being intra-state – *i.e.* civil wars).

All this points to the fact that mankind's attempts to address the 'scourge of war,' as it applies to inter-state war, has for a variety of reasons had some effect. And along the way we have begun to educate ourselves to the fact that intra-state conflicts also represent a threat to peace, as they do to widely held values concerning the right to life.

My second question, as to whether states, and individuals, can be induced to support 'international law' is, therefore, more stringent than it may have seemed to be. For we must ask whether there is support for curtailing the power of the state both in its relations to other states and in its dealings with its own people. The answer to this question is, I believe, to be found in the unprecedented number of requests over the past decade for UN intervention in extreme cases of intra-state violence.

Largely in response to these civil wars the UN, through the General Assembly and the Security Council, became involved in some twenty new peacekeeping operations since 1988, a total exceeding the number in the previous 42 years. At the same time the number of UN peacekeepers rose ten-fold to, at times, in excess of 70,000. Sporadically, the support can be found in the international community, it would seem, for action to moderate both inter-state and intra-state violence.

This discussion leads, therefore, to an affirmative answer to my questions one and two. Even in the realm of war there exists an emerging body of law that transcends the national, and, accompanying that, an increasing desire internationally to see that law enforced.

This ongoing revolution in world-view is in no way surprising. Seen from the vantage point of a technocrat, such as myself, it is an outcome of the huge reach of modern technology which offers us a choice of unprecedented destruction and suffering or unprecedented health and prosperity.

The technocrat's view is, of course, incomplete. No less important is the mounting moral revulsion of an educated populace in the face of cruelty and injustice. However, the technocrat in me is not that easily silenced. The reason that we are so aware of horrors at home and abroad is not only that our ethics have improved, but because modern communications force awareness on us. Technology impacts on ethics. That is, however, a sub-text to this essay.

Given a new willingness to act on the basis of universal principles, how should we seek to do so? This was my third and last question. I answer it in the broadest terms by saying that we must be willing to learn.

One thinks, by analogy, of a larger learning experience; our attempts to prevent crime domestically. The history of these attempts is short. Professional police forces have been around for about two centuries. And they are called 'forces' for a reason. They are organized on the presumption that where peaceful means fail, the use of force, under close supervision and according to principles of law, may be required.

One fundamental guiding principle is that never more than the minimum of force may be used. Another is that the police shall be held accountable for their conduct under the law. Both these principles are designed to make certain that those who wield force as police do so in the service of a duly constituted authority and not on their own behalf. For if they act otherwise they become indistinguishable from those they are intended to police.

After well over a century of refining and applying these principles to our police forces, we are not surprised to find that they fall short of the ideal. Some police are corrupt, some racist, some both. Still more are ineffectual, due to inadequacies that include resources, tactics and training. All this has not led us to disband police forces in favour of anarchy, but to renew our attempts to understand the nature of the task of policing, and then to do it better. The same must apply in the vastly more complex realm of UN peacekeeping.

In *An Agenda for Peace*, published in 1992, the Secretary General of the UN responded to a request from the Security Council (meeting for the first time as heads of state rather than ambassadors) to make recommendations for strengthening the organization's capacity for making and keeping peace. The Secretary General responded with an 'Agenda' that, while it provides work for the coming century, is already helping to clarify thinking.

An Agenda for Peace distinguishes four categories of UN activities on behalf of peace: preventive diplomacy, peacemaking, peacekeeping and peacebuilding.

Preventive diplomacy attempts to bring hostile parties to agreement before conflict leads to war. This as yet poorly developed field includes conflict identification as well as a warning function. Currently the UN Secretariat has inadequate staff in the area of preventive diplomacy. We need to invest much more in preventive diplomacy. The operation of one element in the recent past, the warning function, can perhaps be judged from the fact that the UN Secretariat had to send out for maps showing the Falkland Islands when the Falklands invasion occurred.

Peacemaking makes use of many of the same diplomatic skills as preventive diplomacy, but does so after a dispute has become an armed conflict. The aim, then, is to reduce the intensity of the conflict through negotiation, as a step on the path to a cease-fire.

Peacekeeping involves deployment of armed UN personnel to help defuse a conflict. It differs from peacemaking in one crucial way; the peacekeepers arrive when a cease-fire has been agreed to, with the purpose of seeing that it is honoured.

Peacebuilding, the final category of operation, involves the building of all sorts of structures (such as social services, a judiciary and responsive government) that strengthen peace and order. Peacebuilding can occur before or after a conflict, but is certain to be badly needed in the aftermath of war.

These pedantic categories for UN action are, as can be imagined, both overlapping and incomplete. One thinks of the 1000 person UN force that separates the Kosovo area of Serbia from the former Yugoslav Republic of Macedonia. This UN force is something new. Since armed personnel are involved, it is not preventive diplomacy. For the same reason, and also since there has been no conflict, it cannot be peacemaking. Since there has been no shooting and therefore no cease-fire, it cannot be peacekeeping. By elimination, it must therefore be peacebuilding. Whatever it is, it is sensible and farsighted.

It is evident that there is a broad range of actions before, during and following conflict which the UN, provided with the proper mix of military and civilian personnel, can undertake. None should be neglected.

If one of these categories is to be made flexible so as to cover a spectrum of actions it should be peacekeeping, which has already gone into the language. Two Nobel Peace Prizes have acknowledged that. The institution became tangible one might say on the day in 1956 when, in order to distinguish UN peacekeeping troops in Suez from a large number of others, an unused pile of helmet-liners were painted blue and distributed to the troops to wear. Little by little the blue helmet is taking its place as a symbol of courage and service. This is not to deny that the blue helmets will at times be suspect, or even disgraced. But the symbol must be strong enough to withstand that, and there is, one must hope if one is to believe in the future, a global commitment to make it so.

In recent times we have come to group under the heading of peacekeeping, activities which go beyond the monitoring of a cease-fire to the enforcing of one. We are gradually coming to terms with the fact that our peacekeepers cannot be held hostage to the first malcontent, as would be the case if they were withdrawn if one of the warring parties, as too often happens, decided to violate a cease-fire or attack the UN troops. The right to self-defence on the part of the blue-helmets should be real.

Additionally, the obligation to enforce a cease-fire, rather than merely monitor it, should sometimes be placed upon the peacekeepers. The case for such peace-enforcement will be strong in instances where the UN believes a cease-fire has a chance, and where the international community has the resolve to follow through till the action is made effective.

There are people of good conscience who argue against the use of force by the UN on the grounds that peace cannot come from the barrel of a gun. I respect that viewpoint, but am not persuaded by it. Force, as I have already stressed, should be used according to prescribed guidelines, as a last resort, and to the least extent. It should only be used where there is sufficient local support for a settlement, that success appears possible. But these conditions having been met, it should be used as it would also be used domestically to halt violent crime.

The argument that force inevitably begets force gives too little weight to the difference between legality and illegality, between right and wrong. If a criminal is apprehended in the act of committing a crime, there is an obligation, when exhortation fails, to take action.

In the case of Bosnia, the UN was applying force when it mandated an exclusion zone for heavy weapons around Sarajevo, or instituted 'safe havens' centred on several cities. It then betrayed that trust by failing to respond to Bosnian Serb defiance of these measures. This marked a dramatic change in spirit since the time when General Phillipe Morillon of France, surrounded only by a few (Canadian) peacekeepers, courageously faced down a Serb attack on the haven of Srebrenica with the words; 'A Serb attack on Srebrenica will be an attack on the whole world.' The Serbian forces gave way. Later they did not, for, 'the whole world,' as Morillon described it, had shown its weakness.

This tragic situation is in no sense a death-blow to collective security, nor does it imply that we should abandon the UN. Collective security is, in the long run, the only security on offer. It must be made to work. But we have to accept the obligations that this places on us. And rather than blame the United Nations for weakness, we should blame ourselves, for we are the United Nations.

Our failures can be broken down into the tactical and the strategic. We have much to learn under both headings.

At the level of tactics we should learn that we cannot switch, without risk and cost, from a mission which is humanitarian, to enforcement. Humanitarian activities, in common with monitoring, require lightly-armed forces that are widely dispersed. They are correspondingly vulnerable to attack and to capture.   Any attempt to re-configure the force will be conspicuous, and is liable to be pre-empted by the opposing side.   These are the tactical problems, and they must be addressed.   But it would be ludicrous to suppose that they can lead to the defeat of the world by a rag-tag army.

The strategic problem is, in essence, the one with which I began.   We must commit ourselves more thoroughly to collective security.   This involves the adoption of a longer-range interpretation of the hallowed concept of 'national interest' to include a deeper concern for the viability of the instruments of collective security; the UN, NATO and other regional groupings.   It is not too much to hope that we can set the world more firmly on this course, since history leaves us no other option.

A few years ago President Clinton was pleading for military action to protect the Bosnian haven of Gorazde, on the grounds that this was needed to maintain 'NATO as a credible force for peace in the post Cold War era.'[1]   Clearly he regarded such action in distant places as in the US national interest.   It would not have been necessary to invent such a subtle concept as the 'national interest' if security meant simply the defence of the homeland.   Today the credibility of the UN is of vital interest to any nation that wishes to function in a secure world.   The greater the nation the more zealously it should guard this 'national interest,' since its place of privilege gives it the most to lose from a regime of global anarchy.

New habits, and this is a new habit for the major powers as it is for the world, are not established without difficulty and back-sliding.   We are being asked to make sacrifices in new ways, namely to prevent wars rather than fight them at appalling cost.   We are being asked to develop new institutions.   There have to be sacrifices of traditional prerogatives along the way.   But they must be taken along the path that offers hope, the path mapped in broad terms in the Charter of the United Nations.   The Charter was born of two world wars; history will not forgive us if we wait for a third.

This essay is based on an address made at the opening of the International Peace University, Berlin, September 1, 1995.

Reference

1.   *New York Times*, April 21, 1994.

14

A Bridge to the Twenty-First Century

Sandra J. Ionno

My generation grew up in a hair-trigger world. Tens of thousands of nuclear weapons were poised, ready to wipe away the days of our charmed superpower childhood and we knew nothing about them and other events that were changing the world. Vietnam to me was hushed silences around flashing TV news screens and a defiant orange neon peace sign in my teenage brother's room. I vaguely remember seeing the first moon walk, Nixon resign, and the horrible helicopter crash when President Carter tried to free the hostages. Throughout my primary and secondary education, nuclear weapons barely made it onto my radar screen. I didn't know about MX or Trident missiles. One of my school's top students, I somehow was sixteen before I learned about the Holocaust. I graduated from high school in 1983. President Reagan was warming up, AIDS was breaking out, and my generation began to wake up.

We don't remember the drills, ducking below school desks as my sister recounts. We have no memory of the Cuban Missile Crisis. The Second World War is history to us. Alan Alda taught us about the Korean War through edgy jokes on persistent M*A*S*H re-runs. The TV movie 'The Day After' was our introduction to nuclear weapons. While we always have known it is possible for mankind to destroy this planet – this message seeped into our consciousness from many different sources – we also grew up in an era of unbounded scientific possibility. We are at once sceptics and optimists. We know technology can harm egregiously the world's ecosystems and peoples, yet we still hope science will change the world for the better. We, who don't know how a toaster works, have the utmost faith that our leaders will protect us from Dr. Strangelove's cousins, in whatever labs they may be working.

We will be the bridge between two centuries. A group of overstimulated, under-educated, selfish, at times loving, worldly, avoiders-of-commitment will be the emissaries to a whole new millennium. It is our task to piece together the future from the mixed bag of twentieth century lessons.

We will rely upon the bright vision of those who shaped this century to guide us into these uncharted new scientific and cultural frontiers. Those who have held mankind's future in their hands and who know the weight, texture, and nuance of such responsibility – the bomb makers, policy drivers, and military men and women who would caution us and advise us, must speak loudly and clearly to my generation if they want to be heard through the white noise of youthful distraction. And my peers and I must listen and move forward in conscientious ways.

There is hope that these lessons are being heard and that change is happening. Albert Einstein once wrote:

> ... I believe that older people who have scarcely anything to lose ought to be willing to speak out on behalf of those who are young and who are subject to much greater restraint. I like to think that it may be of some help to them. Strange that science, which in the old days seemed rather harmless, should have evolved into a nightmare that causes everyone to tremble. And fear is the worst counsel of all.[1]

In recent times, eminent men and women have taken to the bully pulpit to speak for disarmament and to encourage sanity in world affairs. Each Robert McNamara, Lee Butler, Stansfield Turner and Joseph Rotblat helps to expand the realm of possibility for my generation with every pronouncement they make.[2] By admitting to us the folly of the world they helped create, they give us license to dismantle its excesses and mistakes, and to do so in a way that allows us to honour their lives.

My generation has not known war (the Persian Gulf War barely affected us). In contrast, my father enlisted to fight in the Second World War when he was 17. He wanted to combat the evil he saw spreading in the world. Shaken by his experiences on the battlefield, he gave up his religion – no priest could provide him with a sufficient answer as to why it was acceptable to kill when ordered to do so by his government. He was in Hiroshima after it was bombed, though in my years of studying nuclear weapons issues he never told me this. When I finally learned about it, I asked him, with a hunger for the knowledge, what it was like. His answer, so insufficient to me at the time, was simply: 'What do you think it was like?' Like so many of his generation, he wanted to protect me from that knowledge. He wanted a better life for me.

But my generation needs to know. We need to know now before we make some very stupid choices. We need to know how to respond to the danger of new weapons of mass destruction and to Dolly, the sheep clone. We need to know what to think about global warming and depleting rain forests. We need to decide soon what will continue to be sacred in a world laid naked by science and technology. And we need heroes to show us by their example that we can find within us the courage to make difficult choices, that it is never too late to do the right thing.

Perhaps nowhere is the need for leadership so great as in today's rapidly evolving world of science and technology. Serguei Kapitza warned of this imperative when he wrote:

> We have to adjust and reorient our educational system in a broad sense to take into account the social consequences of the enormous advances of science and technology; of all global problems the arms race is one of the most conspicuous, costly and inherently dangerous. The history of mankind and the development of man have demonstrated that, on a number of occasions in the past, technical and scientific advances have overtaken social development. Today this gap is so great that the very existence of our future depends on it being closed.[3]

If this gap is to be closed, it will require an intergenerational dialogue so that those who are coming up in the fields will learn from those who appreciate the depth of the choices to be made. But this is too often not the case, as Joseph Rotblat pointed out: 'Many [scientists] are actually opposed to the involvement of scientists with anything they consider to be outside the field of pure science. Worse still, they discourage, or actively hamper, young scientists from being concerned with the social impact of science.'[4] To the contrary, he believes 'it is incumbent on all young scientists to ponder on the implications of their work and ensure responsible use of science and technology.'[5] Rotblat understands the pressures placed upon young scientists:

> 'I've got my job to do; let others worry about the possible consequences of my work,' is the attitude of many young scientists. This is where the social conscience comes in, the conscious effort required to fulfil one's social responsibility. My appeal to young scientists is this: make that effort; devote a small proportion of your time to the social implications of your work; remember that the misuse of science could have a cataclysmic effect on everyone, everywhere.[6]

Bertrand Russell, a leading voice in the early days of the nuclear era, addressed the great progress that can come from individual action in his last essay, written in 1967:

> Any man who cares about what the future has in store ... has to choose
> between nothingness and conciliation, not once, but throughout future ages,
> until the sun grows cold... What can private persons do meanwhile? They
> can agitate by pointing out the effects of modern war and the danger of the
> extinction of Man. They can teach men not to hate peoples other than
> their own, or to cause themselves to be hated. They can value, and cause
> others to value what Man has achieved in art and science. They can
> emphasize the superiority of co-operation to competition. Finally, have I
> done anything to further such ends? Something, perhaps, but sadly little
> in view of the magnitude of the evil. Some few people in England and the
> USA I have encouraged in the expression of liberal views, or have terrified
> with knowledge of what modern weapons can do. It is not much, but if
> everybody did as much, this earth would soon be a paradise.[7]

The lesson to young people should be that it is not necessary to devote
one's whole life to activism. Often, education, awareness and targeted
involvement can make the most profound differences. Another of the
giants of this century, Albert Einstein, remained equally humble in terms
of his contributions:

> In a long life I have devoted all my faculties to reach a somewhat deeper
> insight into the structure of physical reality. Never have I made any
> systematic effort to ameliorate the fortunes of men, to fight injustice and
> oppression, or to improve the traditional forms of human relations. The
> only thing I did was this: At long intervals I have publicly expressed
> opinions on such conditions in society which I considered to be so bad and
> unfortunate that silence would have made me feel guilty of complicity.[8]

This is the challenge for my generation. To have the courage to speak
out when the times demand a response. And to know the value of dialogue
and conciliation in a world too-often polarized. The dangers we face are
very real, as Rotblat points out:

> The nuclear issue is not the only mortal peril we face; our civilization may
> be heading to extinction by yet another consequence of science and
> technology: the steady poisoning of the environment. Whether in a bang
> or with a whimper, civilization will be doomed unless a conscious effort
> is made to save it. It is incumbent on scientists to be in the forefront of
> that effort... [T]his applies both to senior scientists already established in
> their professions, and to the young scientists on the threshold of their
> careers. In choosing a field of work, ethical issues must be given due
> consideration. For some young scientists this may be in the form of a kind
> of Hippocratic Oath. With or without a formal pledge, it is incumbent on
> all young scientists to ponder on the implications of their work and ensure
> responsible use of science and technology.[9]

This idea of a pledge has circulated for many years, with various initiatives gaining different levels of success. During the Reagan years, scientists pledged not to work on any programmes related to the Strategic Defense Initiative, Reagan's technically flawed dream of an 'umbrella' to protect the United States from possible nuclear attack. More recently, Nobel laureate Hans Bethe has urged scientists to pledge not to work on nuclear weapons programmes. Most of these types of initiatives are targeted for very specific purposes and as such do not reach down to very many young people. There have been efforts by some young people to encourage their peers. One limited exercise is the graduation pledge promoted by the Graduate Pledge Alliance in the United States.[10]

There is a new initiative in this regard. In the days after October 13, 1995, when the Norwegian Nobel Committee announced that they would award that year's Nobel Peace Prize to the Pugwash Conferences on Science and World Affairs and to its then-president, Joseph Rotblat, Student Pugwash USA considered how to honour Pugwash's pioneering work. We decided to take Professor Rotblat's idea of a kind of Hippocratic Oath on the responsible use of science and to make it into a reality. This new pledge states:

> I promise to work for a better world, where science and technology are used in socially responsible ways. I will not use my education for any purpose intended to harm human beings or the environment. Throughout my career, I will consider the ethical implications of my work before I take action. While the demands placed upon me may be great, I sign this declaration because I recognize that individual responsibility is the first step on the path to peace.[11]

As of August 1998, this pledge has been signed by over 4500 people in over 50 countries around the world. The pledge hopefully will expand in coming years and will reach into graduation exercises as it gains more prominence. It is one example of the younger generation accepting responsibility for the world to come. According to Rotblat, who inspired this initiative,

> The pledge campaign started with a highly ambitious target: a million signatures by the end of the millennium. It is most unlikely that this target will be achieved, but it expresses the exuberance, the unbounded optimism of the young. We, the older folk, should not attempt to curb this enthusiasm. On the contrary, we should give every help to promote the pledge campaign.[12]

But, such a pledge is only the first step. As Albert Einstein said:

'Mere praise of peace is easy, but ineffective. What is needed is active participation in the fight against war and everything that leads to it.'[13] It requires a lifelong process of commitment and courage, and its success is not always guaranteed nor valued. Einstein thought that this type of individual action would become increasingly important:

> There is ... one human right which, although infrequently mentioned, seems destined to become very important: the individual's right and obligation to abstain from participating in those activities which he considers wrong or pernicious.[14]

It helps young people immeasurably to be able to look to role models when taking this type of isolated, individual, and essential action. It is only through a partnership between experience and optimism, ideals and cynicism, youthful exuberance and aged wisdom that we will be able to fashion a future worthy of our collective talents. Many in my generation may not know war, but in too many places around the world our peers are under siege, fighting for their survival in a world that seems all too ready to pass them by. Shocking as it seems to some, two-thirds of the world's population have never placed a telephone call.[15] We need to think about that before we start planning our travel on the global information superhighway, before we start thinking that the twenty-first century is guaranteed to yield a better life for all people.

It is our privilege as the next generation to capture the best of what has been and to shape it into a future of which we can all be proud. I have seen what is good in my peers and I believe we can rise to the challenge, with help from those whose words and actions can light our way. Please speak to us now, shout if you must. We are listening, though you may not know it. We are ready to carry on.

Professor Rotblat summarized our collective challenge beautifully when he wrote: 'We scientists, young and old, must nurture a vision of a better world in the next century, a world without war, a society based on care and equity, a community that will protect the environment. And we should make it our task to turn this vision into reality.'[16]

Notes and References

1. Albert Einstein, in a letter to the Queen Mother of Belgium, March 28, 1954, two weeks after his 75th birthday, in Otto Nathan and Heinz Norden, *Einstein on Peace,* New York: Avenel Books, 1981, p. 604.

2. Robert McNamara is a former US Secretary of Defense; General Lee Butler is a former head of the US Strategic Air Command; Admiral Stansfield Turner is a former head of the Central Intelligence Agency; and Joseph Rotblat is a former member of the Manhattan Project. All of these men have called for eventual nuclear disarmament.

3. Serguei Kapitza, 'Social consciousness and education for disarmament (how to learn to think in a new way),' *Scientists, the Arms Race and Disarmament*: A UNESCO/Pugwash Symposium, ed. Joseph Rotblat, London: Taylor and Francis, 1982, p. 253.

4. Joseph Rotblat, 'Pugwash – The Social Conscience of Scientists,' Closing Address, 47th Annual Pugwash Conference, Lillehammer, Norway, August 7, 1997.

5. Joseph Rotblat, Preface, *Jobs You Can Live With: Working at the Crossroads of Science, Technology, and Society,* Washington D.C.: Student Pugwash USA, 1996.

6. Joseph Rotblat, interviewed in Student Pugwash USA's newsletter, *Tough Questions*, Summer 1991.

7. Bertrand Russell Archives, McMaster University. www.web.apc.org/~pgs/pages/russell.html, revised 7/28/96.

8. Albert Einstein, in a 'Message on Human Rights,' dated December 5, 1953, played before the Decalogue Society, February 20, 1954, in Otto Nathan and Heinz Norden, *Einstein on Peace*, p. 600.

9. Joseph Rotblat, Preface, *Jobs You Can Live With* ...

10. This pledge states simply: 'I pledge to thoroughly investigate and take into account the social and environmental consequences of any job opportunity I consider.'

11. For more information about this pledge, contact Student Pugwash USA, 815, 15th Street, NW, Suite 814, Washington, DC 20005. Information is also available on the Student Pugwash USA Web site: www.spusa.org/pugwash/.

12. Joseph Rotblat, 'Pugwash – The Social Conscience of Scientists.'

13. Albert Einstein, in a letter to the Jewish Peace Fellowship in NY, September 21, 1953, Otto Nathan and Heinz Norden, *Einstein on Peace*, p. 595.

14. Albert Einstein, in a 'Message on Human Rights,' dated December 5, 1953, played before the Decalogue Society, February 20, 1954, Otto Nathan and Heinz Norden, *Einstein on Peace*, p. 601.

15. Harper's Index, 5/97, quoted in a 1997 brochure by Global Connections: A National Conversation About a Changing World, an initiative of InterAction.

16. Joseph Rotblat, Preface, *Jobs You Can Live With* ...

15

The Social Responsibility of Scientists

Michael Atiyah

Most scientists spend their working life devoted to their subject, impelled by intellectual curiosity and the general cultural appeal of science as a magnificent human enterprise. But events may distract them from their introverted activities and turn their attention to the outside world. Those of Joseph Rotblat's generation could not escape the impact of the Second World War and its aftermath. In my own case, after many years of quiet mathematical research, working out of the limelight, a major change occurred when unexpectedly I found myself president of the Royal Society, in a very public position, and expected to act as a general spokesman for the whole of science.

Faced with this new challenge I asked myself what was the essential function of the Royal Society and what public issues should I, as president, be addressing? Of course this question can be answered in various ways but the answer that I found most appealing, and that has been attributed to one of my predecessors, was that the Royal Society should act as 'the conscience of science.'

During my five years as president I had time to reflect on the meaning of this phrase and how it should be interpreted. This essay gives me the opportunity of sharing my views on what I believe is an important topic. Essentially I want to address the question: Are scientists responsible for the ultimate applications of science, with all its consequences?

Let me first demolish one possible line of defence used by the 'pure scientist' who says: 'I work on basic science, advancing knowledge. It is the engineers or applied scientists who have to worry about the consequences. My conscience is clear.' Those who are fully aware of the intimate links between science and technology are unlikely to be taken in by this specious argument.

If one takes a quick historical look at the evolution of science, the

151

essential links between basic science and its applications are apparent. Euclidean geometry, with its emphasis on axioms and proofs, is often taken as a typical illustration of pure mathematics, but no-one doubts that this emerged from earlier practical experience of the real world. A more doubtful example is provided by the famous sixteenth century astronomer, Tycho Brahe, whose research is reputed to have cost the Danish king ten per cent of the Royal budget. Expenditure on this scale is only justified by practical applications and astronomers in those days justified their keep by predicting heavenly events that would guarantee success in battle!

But it was Francis Bacon who set out the clearest vision of a scientific community that would seek to understand nature for the practical benefit of mankind. This vision was in fact the inspiration that led to the founding of the Royal Society. Incidentally, Bacon thought that some scientific discoveries were too dangerous to be disclosed to the state and should be restricted to the scientific community. This was a far-sighted, if ultimately impracticable, aim.

Some people have argued that despite the Baconian aim of scientists, one should not make exaggerated claims on their behalf and it was really the engineers, the inventors, who led the industrial revolution in the eighteenth and nineteenth centuries. There may be some truth in this assertion but only if one ignores the fact that the engineering of one century is made possible by the intellectual climate created by thinkers of previous centuries. I find it difficult to believe that railway locomotives were entirely uninfluenced by the ideas of Newtonian mechanics.

The pace is speeded up in the twentieth century and the practical consequences of basic science are more evident. The vast electronics and communications industries on which modern society is based are crucially dependent on the work of Faraday and Maxwell. Nuclear energy, which is now a major source of power (and to which I will return) emerged from a thorough understanding of the nature of matter. In the biological field the discovery of the double helix is now bearing practical fruit and will have enormous consequences in the next century.

It is evident that scientific discoveries lead, in the fullness of time, to practical applications in engineering and medicine, affecting the lives of all mankind. A scientist, pursuing research, may be only dimly aware of, or motivated by, the potential consequences. Moreover, each individual contribution to the jig-saw puzzle may not seem so significant. But, taken as a whole, the scientific enterprise has transformed the world and looks set to transform it yet further.

Insofar as the practical applications are beneficial, scientists no doubt take collective pride in their contribution. But, what of the downside?

Should scientists not be prepared to accept a share of the blame for misuse or unfortunate consequences of science?

The orthodox reaction is on the following lines. If scientists in general cannot put the blame on the applied scientists or engineers, because they are too close to them, then the blame must be put on the politicians who make the decisions. Admittedly, in a democracy, politicians theoretically act on behalf of the people and a scientist, in his private capacity as a citizen, can attempt to influence public affairs.

But this attempt to distinguish between the scientist as creative research worker and the scientist as citizen is, I think, too simplistic and too easy an escape. I believe that scientists have a very particular responsibility, well beyond that of the average citizen, in trying to ensure that science is put to the best use and that any harmful consequences are minimized. Let me list the reasons why scientists have a special role and obligation.

1. First there is the argument of moral responsibility. If you create something, you should be concerned with the consequences. This should apply as much to making scientific discoveries as it does to having children.
2. Scientists will understand the technical problems better than the average politician or citizen, and knowledge brings responsibility.
3. Scientists can provide technical advice and assistance for solving the incidental problems that may emerge.
4. Scientists can warn of future dangers that may arise from current discoveries.
5. Scientists form an international fraternity that transcends natural boundaries, so they are well placed to take a global view in the interests of mankind.
6. Finally, there is need to prevent a public backlash against science ('We have to stop these mad scientists from ruining the earth, creating monsters or blowing us all up.') Self-interest requires that scientists must be fully involved in public debate and must not be seen as 'enemies of the people.'

I put this self-interest argument last because it is, I think, lowest on the ethical scale. However, for those whose conscience is elastic, and who are not swayed by broader ethical issues, self-interest can be compelling. Even if you are not an angel at heart it is good public relations to be seen to be on the side of the angels!

For all these reasons, scientists must acquire a social conscience and concern themselves actively with the political process insofar as this relates to the use and misuse of science. In our present complex technologically-based society this is a fairly all-embracing agenda.

The scientist is now a concerned citizen interested in making a contribution to the scientific-political debate. He wants to get involved, make use of his expert knowledge and assist the public. It is great if he is so enthusiastic, but there are a few obstacles to talking freely. There is such a thing as secrecy. Educated and trained in the free climate of a university he will have learnt that the unfettered circulation and publication of ideas is the life-blood of science, that the spread of knowledge is a good thing and that open discussion is the essential criticism that validates scientific truth. He is in for a rude shock. In the real world secrecy is the name of the game. It comes in many forms and is widespread, even in democratic countries.

First, there are military secrets, and a substantial proportion of our scientists and engineers are involved, directly or indirectly, with military research. If the scientist is in this position, he may be well-informed about important matters of public interest but is effectively debarred from taking part in open debate. Even when he has moved on and is no longer directly involved with military matters, his lips are supposed to be sealed. So we have the odd situation where the only people who have sufficient technical knowledge to inform the public are prevented from doing so. It is then hardly surprising if the public is fed on a mixture of government propaganda and media hysteria – a somewhat indigestible combination.

So, as a dedicated scientist and responsible citizen, he decides to keep away from anything military. This may be more difficult than he thinks since his research might in some indirect way be supported by, or of interest to, the military. Still, he perseveres and makes sure that he is employed by a civilian organization, perhaps a pharmaceutical company which aims to preserve people rather than to kill them. It has lofty humanitarian aims. Alas, he soon discovers that secrecy is not the prerogative of the military alone. Commercial secrecy and the struggle for patents are just as potent. 'Publish or perish' may be the slogan in the academic world, but in the competitive commercial market it is more likely to be 'Publish and perish.' He may be a whiz-kid in bio-technology, who could enlighten a much-concerned public about the benefits or dangers of the latest research, but is severely constrained in what he can divulge. Moreover his utterances may be biased by commercial considerations and he is unlikely to be trusted as a source of disinterested information.

If the military and commercial worlds are too obsessed with secrecy then how about entering the public service? Surely, as a servant of the people, he will be free to put his knowledge into the public arena? This is an understandable hope but much too naive. Civil servants are only indirectly responsible to 'the people.' In between come ministers and the government of the day, whose main concern is usually to prevent embarrassment. Scientific truth may not be helpful to government policy and if so it is better suppressed. Civil servants who step out of line do so at their peril and 'acting in the public interest' is not usually accepted as a legal defence.

If all these avenues look unpromising for him as a concerned scientist, then perhaps he has no honourable alternative but to stay in academic life. He can tell his vice-chancellor that he quite likes university life and wants to stay on! Assuming the vice-chancellor is co-operative he is at last free to speak his mind. He can rail against nuclear weapons, the patenting of DNA or the dumping of oil rigs in the North Sea. But he may have to be careful and check who is really funding his research. Universities have to depend on a wide variety of financial sources and the vice-chancellor might get a bit worried if his staff were constantly biting the hand that fed them. He might politely explain how much he sympathized with the views expressed, how determined he was to maintain academic freedom, but perhaps the staff could be a trifle more circumspect in public utterances?

Even if legal inhibitions or financial apron-strings are left out, there are still subtle social pressures that act within the scientific elite. These are most evident in disputes with the environmental movement or with the media and can be described as the 'we know best' syndrome. If there is an official establishment line on a controversial scientific topic, it is regarded as poor form for a scientist to question it openly and side with the opposition. Because protest movements and the popular press, aiming to attract attention, are inclined to exaggerate, there is a tendency to write them off as unworthy of serious consideration. A scientist who ventured, however tentatively, to see merit in their case would be seen by his colleagues as letting the side down and providing succour to the rabble.

Now that I have pointed out the limits of free speech, I turn to matters of substance. What are the major issues that scientists should be concerned about? Which are the areas where the application of science have been harmful and what threats are there in the future that we should try to avoid? It is not hard to identify three main areas where science has had a potentially devastating impact and has left us with vast problems that will dominate the next century.

First, there is the enormous military threat posed by weapons of mass destruction: nuclear, chemical and biological. Not only are these weapons awesome in their destructive power but the scientific contribution is unambiguous. There may not be much science in bows and arrows but there certainly is in the atomic bomb.

The second potential catastrophe that can, indirectly at least, be laid at the door of science is the population explosion of the world. Improving health care and the elimination of many diseases are the benefits of medical research. The reduction in child mortality and the dramatic increase in life expectancy are great humanitarian triumphs. But the resulting rapid growth of the world population presents us with a major problem. The social, economic and environmental stresses that this has produced are all too evident and we are rapidly approaching the limit that the earth can sustain.

Finally, there is the general degradation of the environment arising out of the improved lifestyle that science and technology have made possible. The motor car is perhaps the most obvious symbol. A great asset to each individual, allowing for mobility and convenience, but collectively an environmental disaster polluting our air and clogging up our streets. Of course the population explosion accentuates the environmental problem and can be viewed as part of it.

It is hard to deny that these great problems are the major issues facing mankind as we come to the end of the remarkable twentieth century. It is also hard to deny the role that science has played in creating them. What is surprising and a little depressing is that they appear to be almost entirely ignored by Western politicians in their election campaigns. It is a sad reflection of the democratic process. But it is the responsibility of scientists to keep reminding their fellow citizens of the fundamental problems that the world faces, as opposed to the petty parochial problems that attract all their attention. Let me consider in more detail the problem of nuclear weapons since they still represent the greatest threat to all of us. It may be helpful to review their history over the past fifty-odd years.

As is well known, the first moves came from leading scientists. After the initial work by Otto Hahn in 1939, showing that bombardment by neutrons could split an atom of uranium, Frisch and Peierls in Britain and Einstein and Szilard in the United States wrote to their respective governments, pointing out the military implications. Incidentally it is an amusing reflection on British bureaucracy that, as 'enemy aliens' Frisch and Peierls were not, at first, allowed to see the top-secret correspondence that their move had generated.

The subsequent history of the Manhattan Project at Los Alamos, leading to the atomic bombs over Hiroshima and Nagasaki, is well-known and the moral dilemma faced by the scientists involved has also received much attention. As long as there was a significant possibility that the Germans or Japanese might succeed in producing atomic weapons it seemed inevitable that Britain and the United States should press ahead. But by 1944 it was clear that the German effort was too little and too late to affect the course of the war and the Japanese were even further behind. This was the signal that led Joseph Rotblat to withdraw from the project and devote himself to more peaceful science.

For several years after the end of the Second World War there were serious attempts to grapple with the atomic threat, but mutual suspicion at the international level prevented any agreement. This failure triggered the stupendous arms race that followed in which other aspects of science and technology added to the nuclear threat. Missile technology, combined with the power of modern computers and telecommunications, produced the ultimate weapons that could destroy the entire world at the push of a button.

Perhaps the politicians and the generals must take the main blame, but many scientists and engineers were eager partners. It was a distinguished physicist, Edward Teller, who was the prime mover behind the hydrogen bomb and who constantly urged the military establishment to press ahead with the latest technology. It was scientists who were pressing for the anti-ballistic missile defence system that acquired the notorious title of Star Wars.

I am sure that the scientists involved thought they were acting in the national interest, enhancing security and deterring enemies. But it has to be acknowledged that, to the outsider, the scientific advice and encouragement of more and more sophisticated military programmes could be seen as self-serving. It gave scientists status, prestige and resources. A lot of excellent scientific research was funded through the largesse of the US defence department budget, and it required considerable self-denial to turn down such support. I am glad that in Britain many scientists publicly refused to accept US research funding in aid of Star Wars, despite considerable pressure and encouragement from the government. This shows that it is possible for scientists to make a stand on moral principles and it is important, for the public perception, that they are seen to be doing so.

So the arms race continued with a build up of nuclear weapons which, a few years ago, had an explosive power equivalent to two tons of TNT for each of the world's inhabitants. If only a small fraction of these weapons had ever been used, the destruction of Hiroshima would have paled into insignificance. If the human race survives well into the next millennium, people will look back on the latter part of the twentieth century as the time when we came closest to collective suicide.

Fortunately we seem to be moving in the right direction. As a result of various international agreements, painstakingly negotiated over many years, and proceeding much more rapidly in the past decade, many types of nuclear weapons are being dismantled. In a few years' time the total stock of such weaponry will be one-fifth of what it was at its peak.

Although the political changes in Europe, beginning with Gorbachev and progressing to the break up of the Soviet Union, have made the task much easier, the initial moves came at a more difficult time when political antagonisms were still deep. I am glad to say that these complex negotiations involved many scientists, some of whom worked through the Pugwash Conferences which fittingly shared the Nobel Peace Prize with its President Joseph Rotblat. One of these was the late Sir Rudolf Peierls, my colleague for many years at Oxford and one of those who initiated the development of nuclear weapons: a fine example of someone whose conscience stirred him into action.

Because of the progress that has been made in reducing stockpiles of nuclear weapons and because of the changed political climate, there is a tendency to become complacent. Nuclear weapons have disappeared from the headlines and are not seen by most people as an imminent threat. But the nuclear weapons that still exist remain a vast potential danger and those who are more far-sighted are urging further action at the present time, while the political tensions are low. The Canberra Commission, an international group of distinguished and experienced people including politicians, generals and scientists, has produced a report arguing for a substantial programme that should aim at the total elimination of nuclear weapons. This is not the report of a group of woolly-headed idealists. The Commission contained figures like Robert McNamara (former US Secretary of Defence) and General Lee Butler (former Commander of the US Nuclear Deterrent). Its proposals are measured and realistic and set out a framework that could eventually eliminate the possibility of nuclear catastrophe. It is an important document that will, I hope, engage the attention of our political leaders when they turn their minds to serious business.

I once spent a sabbatical term as a visitor at the Enrico Fermi Institute in Chicago. Fermi was a great physicist who pioneered experiments in nuclear fission. My office in the Institute named after him looked out onto a square which contained the powerful sculpture, by Henry Moore, of the mushroom cloud which depicted and came to symbolize the atomic bomb. Those of my generation have lived in the shadow of that cloud most of their lives and we should do all that we can to lift it from the lives of succeeding generations.

When alluding to weapons of mass destruction, I mentioned chemical and biological weapons as well as nuclear weapons. Clearly all these are based on science, and scientists are heavily involved with them at all stages. Fortunately the world has already stepped back from the brink on chemical and biological weapons. There are now international treaties that ban their use, and countries that possess stockpiles have undertaken to destroy them. There are plans for control and verification that are designed to stop any clandestine research or production. Unfortunately these sort of checks are difficult to carry out, as is seen in Iraq. The facilities that are required for military purposes are not so different from those for normal commercial use. Unlike nuclear weapons very large scale laboratories are not needed and so external identification is harder. Moreover the kind of research that is needed for peaceful purposes in the chemical or pharmaceutical industry is sometimes difficult to separate from that which may have military applications.

Scientists, as the only ones who thoroughly understand the technicalities, have been closely involved in drawing up the complicated international conventions on chemical and biological weapons. Moreover they will constantly be needed in the future monitoring of these conventions. It is not only as official inspectors that scientists will have to be on the alert. The world is too big a place to be adequately supervised, in the necessary detail, by armies of inspectors. We shall have to rely on individual 'whistle-blowers,' scientists who suspect that conventions are being broken and who bring the matter to international attention. This also applies to nuclear weapons, at least to small-scale infringements that are difficult to detect.

This 'whistle-blowing' role for the individual scientist, in the capacity of a world citizen depends, of course, on a legal and social framework in which such activities are tolerated. As I have already argued, not many countries, even democratic ones, allow their citizens the necessary freedom of speech. The leaking of state secrets may incur severe penalties, even if the leak uncovers activities that are contraventions of international obligations.

A citizen's conscience may impel him or her to break the laws of the country if it is in the wider international interest, but not all of us wish to be martyrs and we should press for the necessary protection of those who are trying to get their own governments to abide by international agreements. More generally there should be a clear 'public interest' defence for those accused of disclosing information. Scientists who are after all in the business of creating and disseminating knowledge should be in the forefront of those demanding greater freedom of speech.

Although weapons of mass destruction provide the extreme test of the scientific conscience, one can hardly turn a blind eye to the role of science in other aspects of warfare. It was presumably a chemist who invented napalm, an efficient device for burning people alive and far more sophisticated than the primitive bonfire at the stake that was used in medieval times. Anti-personnel mines are another of our great inventions, designed to blow the limbs off the rash intruder. Moreover, ingenious scientists have produced mines that traditional devices fail to detect, making them a permanent hazard long after the official conflict has ceased. Princess Diana highlighted this continuing tragedy and her campaign brought added pressure on all countries to ban the use or sale of such mines.

These are just two examples of new weapons produced by our scientists which, by their nature, stir our consciences. But the whole arms industry, with its constant search for new and more deadly weapons is one that intimately involves a large part of the scientific community and poses serious moral questions. The countries of the world spend vast amounts on the military, diverting resources from more essential purposes. This is bad enough in advanced industrial countries where, as we hear every day, essential services in health and education are under a constant squeeze. But it is infinitely worse in the poorer parts of the world where the bare essentials of life are lacking, where the majority of the population are under-nourished and in bad health, and yet their governments continue to buy sophisticated and expensive military hardware.

It is the international arms trade, in which the wealthy countries of the world export their weapons to poor countries that can ill afford them, that should trouble our consciences. In fact the evils of the arms trade and the way this fuels trouble in many parts of the world is so well-known, and so frequently brought home to us on our TV screens, that one might wonder why it survives. Surely the enlightened citizens of the wealthier countries of the world could collectively ban or control the export of arms?

The trouble is that, as with all real ethical problems, our conscience is subverted by what we see (perhaps wrongly) as our self-interest. The arms industries, involved in developing hi-tech expensive weapons, need large markets to cover their costs, and international competition is still a major factor. Western governments look further afield and try to foist their armaments on former colonies or other countries in their sphere of influence. In this competition it clearly helps to have client states which are tied by a combination of factors: historical, economic and political. Many of these countries may be run by cliques or oligarchies whose power and continued existence depend on our support.

From time to time such matters make the newspaper headlines: a major deal to sell hundreds of tanks or aeroplanes is about to be clinched, a Foreign Minister flies out to help the process and to guarantee jobs. The ethics of the sale are secondary, the focus is all on the employment prospects and the financial benefits. Occasionally, some minor criticisms appear about the human rights record of the regime involved or its treatment of ethnic minorities, but these are invariably over-ridden by appeals to national interest. The current British government is addressing the problems of the arms trade and its foreign policy is supposed to have an ethical dimension. It remains to be seen how far this can effectively be implemented.

The scientist employed, directly or indirectly, by the armaments industry may feel uncomfortable with the ultimate destination of what he or she works on, but as a pawn in the whole process it is difficult to see what can be done. One could resolutely keep away from any military contracts, but in certain fields it is hard to disentangle research into separate civilian and military compartments. If one is doing research on computers or telecommunications it is unlikely that there are no military ramifications.

All of this highlights the degree to which scientists have been absorbed into the military-industrial complex. It was Eisenhower, a general turned politician, who coined this phrase and he clearly knew what he was talking about. He was identifying the intricate web that links military needs with the industrial infrastructure, and scientists are right at the core of that link.

Of course science benefits enormously from the support it gets from military and industrial quarters. In some areas it may be almost totally dependent on this patronage. Not only does it finance research but it also enhances the status and self-esteem of the scientists concerned. We all like to feel important and there is nothing like a few files marked Top Secret to raise one's ego.

But there is a price to be paid for this cosy relation between the scientific community and the military-industrial complex. First there is the strain put on one's conscience by being in such doubtful company and conniving at undesirable practices. Second, and just as important, is the loss of independence entailed and the tarnishing of the scientific image in the eyes of the public. On the one hand scientists like to say that science is about the search for truth for the benefit of mankind. On the other scientists are seen arm in arm with those who deal with secrecy, death and destruction. Thus scientists are likely to lose credibility and popularity, making it more difficult for them to play a proper role in society.

There are many other areas where science is involved and where scientists have to examine their conscience. The military case is the most extreme but the relation between science and industry also produces tensions in other areas. I have identified the environmental and pollution problems as another major source of concern. Science has initiated the technology which, as a by-product, has degraded our environment and, to put it bluntly, it is up to scientists to clear up the mess.

Consider for example nuclear power. In many ways this is an ideal way of dealing with our energy needs on a basis that is sustainable on a long time-scale and also does not threaten us with global warming. Yet, in most countries, plans for nuclear power plants have been drastically cut back in the face of public opposition. Why is this? The official establishment view is that the Green movement has misled the public by ill-informed criticism, fanning the flames of suspicion: a few nuclear accidents, notably Chernobyl, have been seized on and grossly exaggerated and a great scientific and technological opportunity has been lost because unscrupulous agitators have played on the fears of the public. There is some truth in this picture but what it ignores is the degree to which the public has lost faith in the scientific community. Because of their involvement with the military, with government and with industry, scientists are not trusted. Past secrecy, or lack of openness, makes scientists suspect and produces hostility. Assertions of safety are not easily accepted.

It also has to be said that there are technological problems in the disposal of nuclear waste that have not yet been solved and are a major embarrassment for the nuclear industry and there is still great controversy about the long-term safety of burying medium level nuclear waste in deep rock deposits and all plans are being subjected to careful scrutiny.

Because of the long lifetimes of some of the radioactive material, there are concerns about the possible pollution of ground water by seepage from the buried waste, over periods of many thousands of years. This means, for example, that one has to worry about the geological effect of the next ice age. Given the complex problems of chemistry, geology and fluid flow involved, it is difficult to see how one can have great confidence in predictions over the necessary timescales. One does not need to be a radical environmentalist to question the long-term outcome.

Although it is difficult to predict physical processes over say 100,000 years, it seems by comparison rather easy to predict that in 100 years' time we shall know a lot more science, and have better ideas on how to dispose of the awkward nuclear waste. On these grounds alone it has always seemed to me that the deep disposal of nuclear waste ought to be in retrievable form so that our successors can extract it easily if they have a better idea. This seems to be a case where it is better to acknowledge inherent scientific uncertainty and plan accordingly.

Problems of the environment, including those arising from the growth of world population, may have their origins in science, and science has much to contribute to their solution. But the problems are vast and complex, involving economic, social and political issues. The scientist can only hope to affect the outcome by participating in the political process. Only the scientist has the relevant technical knowledge to analyse the problems and propose solutions, but it is not easy to operate in the public limelight and under the intense pressures that can be brought to bear.

Perhaps I can illustrate this from my personal experience. A few years ago, while I was president of the Royal Society, I was invited to address the annual lunch of the Parliamentary and Scientific Committee, an event attended by several hundred people including ministers and leaders of industry. I took the opportunity for arguing the case for a ban on tobacco advertising, in the interests of public health and particularly in the interests of the younger generation who are most at risk. After the lunch one of my more experienced colleagues congratulated me on 'a brave speech.' I did not consider I had been particularly brave, but that was due to naivety. Over the next few weeks I was subjected to a campaign of vilification by the tobacco industry who claimed that I had demeaned the role of president of the Royal Society by distorting the evidence. In fact I had taken care to consult my statistical colleagues and I was fully aware of the sophistry being put out by the advertising lobby. For many decades the tobacco industry has been spending vast sums advertising its case, ignoring scientific evidence and exerting pressure on those in power. I was simply the latest in a long line of those to be exposed to this force. For a scientist to be involved in the political process is not easy. There are pressures from many directions and truth is a frequent casualty. But one cannot escape the realities and one has to be prepared to argue one's case robustly.

To sum up: because science has produced such drastic changes in all our lives, scientists have a moral obligation to be concerned. We should try to ensure that science is not misused and we should try to find solutions to the incidental unfortunate by-products of scientific progress. I may have painted an unduly bleak picture of the difficulties that scientists face: the secrecy, the malevolent forces, the hysterical media and the ill-informed public. But the task is not hopeless.

As a top priority I put freedom of information and the elimination of secrecy. Science is inherently about discovering and disseminating the truth and anything that hinders that should be opposed. Next, I urge scientists to cultivate the media. There is an increasing number of intelligent scientifically-trained journalists and broadcasters who can help to inform the public, acting as a bridge to the scientific community. They have a difficult role to perform since their editors may prefer the controversial headline to the measured argument, but that is no reason for the journalists to be spurned or vilified by the scientific community. Both have a common objective in seeing that scientific issues are properly presented to the public.

In referring to malevolent forces and in my digression on the tobacco industry I may have implied that all industrialists are villains and our natural enemies. That is not so. There are many enlightened chief executives who realize that the public interest is not necessarily incompatible with the company's interest, provided one takes a broad enough point of view. On the other hand the institutional and commercial pressures make their task difficult and they need allies from outside, including scientists.

Finally I come to the ill-informed public – in other words 'the people.' There are certainly times when popular movements, fanned by ignorance, mis-information or bigotry, appear hostile to science or to the commercial applications of science. Scientists have to counter the ignorance as best they can and to harness public opinion in constructive directions. There are powerful vested interests in government and industry that will only respond to substantial popular pressure. This is entirely appropriate in a democratic society and provides a counterweight to bureaucratic and financial power. Scientists should have the people on their side.

———————

This essay draws on the Schrödinger Lecture given at Imperial College, London, March 1997.

16

Remember your Humanity

Joseph Rotblat

At this momentous event in my life – the acceptance of the Nobel Peace Prize – I want to speak as a scientist, but also as a human being. From my earliest days I had a passion for science. But science, the exercise of the supreme power of the human intellect, was always linked in my mind with benefit to people. I saw science as being in harmony with humanity. I did not imagine that the second half of my life would be spent on efforts to avert a mortal danger to humanity created by science.

The practical release of nuclear energy was the outcome of many years of experimental and theoretical research. It had great potential for the common good. But the first the general public learned about this discovery was the news of the destruction of Hiroshima by the atom bomb. A splendid achievement of science and technology had turned malign. Science became identified with death and destruction.

It is painful to me to admit that this depiction of science was deserved. The decision to use the atom bomb on Japanese cities, and the consequent build up of enormous nuclear arsenals, was made by governments, on the basis of political and military perceptions. But scientists on both sides of the iron curtain played a very significant role in maintaining the momentum of the nuclear arms race throughout the four decades of the Cold War.

The role of scientists in the nuclear arms race was expressed bluntly by Lord Zuckerman, for many years Chief Scientific Adviser to the British Government:

> When it comes to nuclear weapons ... it is the man in the laboratory who at the start proposes that for this or that arcane reason it would be useful to improve an old or to devise a new nuclear warhead. It is he, the technician, not the commander in the field, who is at the heart of the arms race.

Long before the terrifying potential of the arms race was recognized, there was a widespread instinctive abhorrence of nuclear weapons, and a strong desire to get rid of them. Indeed, the very first resolution of the General Assembly of the United Nations – adopted unanimously – called for the elimination of nuclear weapons. But the world was then polarized by the bitter ideological struggle between East and West. There was no chance to meet this call. The chief task was to stop the arms race before it brought utter disaster. However, after the collapse of communism and the disintegration of the Soviet Union, any rationale for having nuclear weapons disappeared. The quest for their total elimination could be resumed. But the nuclear powers still cling tenaciously to their weapons.

Let me remind you that nuclear disarmament is not just an ardent desire of the people, as expressed in many resolutions of the United Nations. It is a legal commitment by the five official nuclear states, entered into when they signed the Non-Proliferation Treaty. Only a few months ago, when the indefinite extension of the Treaty was agreed, the nuclear powers committed themselves again to complete nuclear disarmament. This is still their declared goal. But the declarations are not matched by their policies, and this divergence seems to be intrinsic.

Since the end of the Cold War the two main nuclear powers have begun to make big reductions in their nuclear arsenals. Each of them is dismantling about 2000 nuclear warheads a year. If this programme continued, all nuclear warheads could be dismantled in little over ten years from now. We have the technical means to create a nuclear-weapon-free world in about a decade. Alas, the present programme does not provide for this. When the START II treaty has been implemented – and remember it has not yet been ratified – we will be left with some 15,000 nuclear warheads, active and in reserve. Fifteen thousand weapons with an average yield of 20 Hiroshima bombs.

Unless there is a change in the basic philosophy, we will not see a reduction of nuclear arsenals to zero for a very long time, if ever. The present basic philosophy is nuclear deterrence. This was stated clearly in the US Nuclear Posture Review which concluded: 'Post-Cold War environment requires nuclear deterrence,' and this is echoed by other nuclear states. Nuclear weapons are kept as a hedge against some unspecified dangers.

This policy is simply an inertial continuation from the Cold War era. The Cold War is over but Cold War thinking survives. Then, we were told that a world war was prevented by the existence of nuclear weapons. Now, we are told that nuclear weapons prevent all kinds of war. These are arguments that purport to prove a negative. I am reminded of a story told in my boyhood, at the time when radio communication began:

Two wise men were arguing about the ancient civilization in their respective countries. One said: 'my country has a long history of technological development: we have carried out deep excavations and found a wire, which shows that already in the old days we had the telegraph.' The other man retorted: 'we too made excavations; we dug much deeper than you and found ... nothing, which proves that already in those days we had wireless communication!'

There is no direct evidence that nuclear weapons prevented a world war. Conversely, it is known that they nearly caused one. The most terrifying moment in my life was October 1962, during the Cuban Missile Crisis. I did not know all the facts – we have learned only recently how close we were to war – but I knew enough to make me tremble. The lives of millions of people were about to end abruptly; millions of others were to suffer a lingering death; much of our civilization was to be destroyed. It all hung on the decision of one man, Nikita Khrushchev: would he or would he not yield to the US ultimatum? This is the reality of nuclear weapons: they may trigger a world war; a war which, unlike previous ones, destroys all of civilization.

As for the assertion that nuclear weapons prevent wars, how many more wars are needed to refute this argument? Tens of millions have died in the many wars that have taken place since 1945. In a number of them nuclear states were directly involved. In two they were actually defeated. Having nuclear weapons was of no use to them.

To sum up, there is no evidence that a world without nuclear weapons would be a dangerous world. On the contrary, it would be a safer world, as I will show later.

We are told that the possession of nuclear weapons – in some cases even the testing of these weapons – is essential for national security. But this argument can be made by other countries as well. If the militarily most powerful – and least threatened – states need nuclear weapons for their security, how can one deny such security to countries that are truly insecure? The present nuclear policy is a recipe for proliferation. It is a policy for disaster.

To prevent this disaster – for the sake of humanity – we must get rid of all nuclear weapons.

Achieving this goal will take time, but it will never happen unless we make a start. Some essential steps towards it can be taken now. Several studies, and a number of public statements by senior military and political personalities, testify that – except for disputes between the present nuclear states – all military conflicts, as well as threats to peace, can be dealt with using conventional weapons. This means that the only function of nuclear weapons, while they exist, is to deter a nuclear attack. All nuclear weapon states should now recognize that this is so, and declare – in treaty form – that they will never be the first to use nuclear weapons. This would open the way to the gradual, mutual reduction of nuclear arsenals, down to zero. It would also open the way for a Nuclear Weapons Convention. This would be universal – it would prohibit all possession of nuclear weapons.

We will need to work out the necessary verification system to safeguard the Convention. A Pugwash study produced suggestions on these matters. The mechanism for negotiating such a convention already exists. Entering into negotiations does not commit the parties. There is no reason why they should not begin now. If not now, when?

So I ask the nuclear powers to abandon the out-of-date thinking of the Cold War period and take a fresh look. Above all, I appeal to them to bear in mind the long-term threat that nuclear weapons pose to humankind and to begin action towards their elimination. Remember your duty to humanity.

My second appeal is to my fellow scientists. I described earlier the disgraceful role played by a few scientists, caricatured as 'Dr Strangeloves,' in fuelling the arms race. They did great damage to the image of science.

On the other side there are the scientists, in Pugwash and other bodies, who devote much of their time and ingenuity to averting the dangers created by advances in science and technology. However, they embrace only a small part of the scientific community. I want to address the scientific community as a whole.

You are doing fundamental work, pushing forward the frontiers of knowledge, but often you do it without giving much thought to the impact of your work on society. Precepts such as 'science is neutral' or 'science has nothing to do with politics,' still prevail. They are remnants of the ivory tower mentality, although the ivory tower was finally demolished by the Hiroshima bomb.

Here, for instance, is a question: Should any scientist work on the development of weapons of mass destruction? A clear 'no' was the answer recently given by Hans Bethe. Professor Bethe, a Nobel laureate, is the most senior of the surviving members of the Manhattan Project. On the occasion of the 50th Anniversary of Hiroshima, he issued a statement that I will quote in full:

> As the Director of the Theoretical Division of Los Alamos, I participated at the most senior level in the World War II Manhattan Project that produced the first atomic weapons.
>
> Now, at age 88, I am one of the few remaining such senior persons alive. Looking back at the half century since that time, I feel the most intense relief that these weapons have not been used since the Second

World War, mixed with the horror that tens of thousands of such weapons have been built since that time – one hundred times more than any of us at Los Alamos could ever have imagined.

Today we are rightly in an era of disarmament and dismantlement of nuclear weapons. But in some countries nuclear weapons development still continues. Whether and when the various Nations of the World can agree to stop this is uncertain. But individual scientists can still influence this process by withholding their skills.

Accordingly, I call on all scientists in all countries to cease and desist from work creating, developing, improving and manufacturing further nuclear weapons – and, for that matter, other weapons of potential mass destruction such as chemical and biological weapons.

If all scientists heeded this call there would be no more new nuclear warheads; no French scientists at Mururoa; no new chemical and biological poisons. The arms race would be over.

But there are other areas of scientific research that may directly or indirectly lead to harm to society. This calls for constant vigilance. The purpose of some governmental or industrial research is sometimes concealed, and misleading information is presented to the public. It should be the duty of scientists to expose such malfeasance. 'Whistle-blowing' should become part of the scientist's ethos. This may bring reprisals; a price to be paid for one's convictions. The price may be very heavy, as illustrated by the disproportionately severe punishment of Mordechai Vanunu. I believe he has suffered enough.

The time has come to formulate guidelines for the ethical conduct of scientists, perhaps in the form of a voluntary Hippocratic Oath. This would be particularly valuable for young scientists when they embark on a scientific career. The US Student Pugwash Group has taken up this idea – and that is very heartening.

At a time when science plays such a powerful role in the life of society, when the destiny of the whole of mankind may hinge on the results of scientific research, it is incumbent on all scientists to be fully conscious of that role, and conduct themselves accordingly. I appeal to my fellow scientists to remember their responsibility to humanity.

My third appeal is to my fellow citizens in all countries: Help us to establish lasting peace in the world.

I have to bring to your notice a terrifying reality: with the development of nuclear weapons Man has acquired, for the first time in history, the technical means to destroy the whole of civilization in a single act. Indeed, the whole human species is endangered, by nuclear weapons or by other means of wholesale destruction which further advances in science are likely to produce.

I have argued that we must eliminate nuclear weapons. While this would remove the immediate threat, it will not provide permanent security. Nuclear weapons cannot be disinvented. The knowledge of how to make them cannot be erased. Even in a nuclear-weapon-free world, should any of the great powers become involved in a military confrontation, they would be tempted to rebuild their nuclear arsenals. That would still be a better situation than the one we have now, because the rebuilding would take a considerable time, and in that time the dispute might be settled. A nuclear-weapon-free world would be safer than the present one. But the danger of the ultimate catastrophe would still be there.

The only way to prevent it is to abolish war altogether. War must cease to be an admissible social institution. We must learn to resolve our disputes by means other than military confrontation.

This need was recognized forty years ago when we said in the Russell-Einstein Manifesto:

> Here then is the problem which we present to you, stark and dreadful, and inescapable: shall we put an end to the human race: or shall mankind renounce war?

The abolition of war is also the commitment of the nuclear weapon states: Article VI of the NPT calls for a treaty on general and complete disarmament under strict and effective international control.

Any international treaty entails some surrender of national sovereignty, and is generally unpopular. As we said in the Russell-Einstein Manifesto: 'The abolition of war will demand distasteful limitations of national sovereignty.'

Whatever system of governance is eventually adopted, it is important that it carries the people with it. We need to convey the message that safeguarding our common property, humankind, will require developing in each of us a new loyalty: a loyalty to mankind. It calls for the nurturing of a feeling of belonging to the human race. We have to become world citizens.

Notwithstanding the fragmentation that has occurred since the end of the Cold War, and the many wars for recognition of national or ethnic identities, I believe that the prospects for the acceptance of this new loyalty are now better than at the time of the Russell-Einstein Manifesto. This is so largely because of the enormous progress made by science and technology during these forty years. The fantastic advances in communication and transportation have shrunk our globe. All the nations of the world have become close neighbours. Modern information techniques enable us to learn instantly about every event in every part of the globe. We can talk to each other via the various networks. This facility will improve enormously with time, because the achievements so far have only scratched the surface. Technology is driving us together. In many ways we are becoming like one family.

In advocating the new loyalty to mankind I am not suggesting that we give up national loyalties. Each of us has loyalties to several groups – from the smallest, the family, to the largest, at present, the nation. Many of these groups provide protection for their members. With the global threats resulting from science and technology, the whole of humankind now needs protection. We have to extend our loyalty to the whole of the human race.

What we are advocating in Pugwash, a war-free world, will be seen by many as a Utopian dream. It is not Utopian. There already exist in the world large regions, for example, the European Union, within which war is inconceivable. What is needed is to extend these to cover the world's major powers.

In any case, we have no choice. The alternative is unacceptable. Let me quote the last sentence of the Russell-Einstein Manifesto:

> We appeal, as human beings, to human beings: Remember your humanity and forget the rest. If you can do so, the way lies open to a new paradise; if you cannot, there lies before you the risk of universal death.

The quest for a war-free world has a basic purpose: survival. But if in the process we learn how to achieve it by love rather than by fear, by kindness rather than by compulsion; if in the process we learn to combine the essential with the enjoyable, the expedient with the benevolent, the practical with the beautiful, this will be an extra incentive to embark on this great task.

Above all, remember your humanity.

Index